Title:

Echoes of the Heart:

"A Journey Through Addiction and Redemption"

Echoes of The Heart

C.W. Fortney

Published by C.W. Fortney, 2024.

ECHOES OF THE HEART

First edition. April 1, 2024.

ISBN: 979-8224669530

Written by C.W. Fortney.

Also by C.W. Fortney

The Core of The Human Heart
The AI ERA & Humanities 2024
AI & The Tapestry of Life
The Journey of The Heart
THE COMPUTER MAN 2024
Tech Titan
Echoes of The Heart
Harmony Nurturing Earth and Humanity

To all who suffer froman addiction that hurts them

In "Echoes of the Heart: A Journey Through Addiction and Redemption," readers are transported into a world where the raw complexities of addiction are met with the unyielding power of love and resilience. Through the intertwining narratives of Mia, Liam, and Gabriel, this captivating tale delves deep into the human psyche, exploring the depths of despair and the heights of redemption.

Mia, a talented artist grappling with the demons of addiction, serves as the anchor of the story. Her journey from the depths of despair to the shores of redemption is a testament to the human spirit's capacity for transformation. As readers witness Mia's struggles and triumphs, they are reminded of the inherent strength that resides within each of us—a strength that can overcome even the most daunting of challenges.

But Mia's journey is not one traveled alone. Alongside her stands Liam, a compassionate therapist whose own battles with addiction lend him a unique perspective. With unwavering support and empathy, Liam guides Mia through the tumultuous waters of recovery, offering her the tools she needs to reclaim her life and rediscover her sense of self-worth.

Enter Gabriel, a charismatic musician whose presence ignites a spark of hope in Mia's heart. Yet, as their bond deepens, Mia is forced to confront the harsh realities of addiction and the toll it takes on those we love. Through Gabriel's eyes, readers are given a glimpse into the complexities of addiction—the highs and lows, the moments of clarity and the lapses into darkness.

As Mia's journey unfolds, "Echoes of the Heart" serves as a poignant reminder of the transformative power of love

In a world where the shadows of addiction loom large, "Echoes of the Heart" illuminates the trans formative power of love, resilience, and the indomitable human spirit. Set against the backdrop of a bustling metropolis, our story follows the intertwined lives of three individuals whose paths converge in the most unexpected of ways. At the center of our tale is Mia, a fiercely independent artist grappling with the demons of addiction. Haunted by past traumas and numbing her pain with alcohol, Mia's once-vibrant spirit is shrouded in darkness. But beneath the surface lies a flicker of hope—a yearning for connection and a longing to reclaim her lost sense of self. Enter Liam, a compassionate therapist whose own struggles with addiction have shaped his understanding of human frailty. Drawn to Mia's vulnerability, Liam becomes her guiding light, offering her the support and empathy she so desperately craves. Together, they embark on a journey of healing and self-discovery, navigating the treacherous waters of addiction with courage and determination. But their world is rocked by the arrival of Gabriel, a charismatic musician with a troubled past of his own. As Gabriel's music weaves its spell over Mia, she finds herself torn between the allure of his carefree lifestyle and the stability offered by Liam's unwavering support.

As Mia grapples with her inner turmoil, she is confronted with the harsh realities of addiction—a cycle of highs and lows, moments of clarity followed by lapses into darkness. But with Liam by her side, she begins to unravel the tangled web of her past, confronting long-buried traumas and finding solace in the power of forgiveness.

Meanwhile, Gabriel's presence serves as a catalyst for change, challenging Mia to confront her demons head-on and reclaim control of her destiny. Yet, as their bond deepens, Mia is forced to confront the painful truth: that love alone may not be enough to overcome the grip of addiction.

As Mia's journey unfolds, "Echoes of the Heart" explores the complex interplay between addiction and the human heart—the ache of longing, the ecstasy of connection, and the enduring hope for redemption. Through moments of triumph and despair, Mia discovers that true healing lies not in escaping her past, but in embracing it with courage and compassion.

Ultimately, "Echoes of the Heart" is a testament to the resilience of the human spirit—a reminder that even in our darkest moments, we possess the strength to rise above our circumstances and forge a path toward redemption. And as Mia's story unfolds, readers are invited to embark on their own journey of self-discovery, finding solace and inspiration in the universal truths that bind us all together.

As readers turn the final page of "Echoes of the Heart," they are left with a profound sense of hope—that no matter how far we may stray from the path, the light of love and redemption will always guide us home. And with AIERA2024.com, readers can continue to explore the themes of addiction, resilience, and the human heart, forging connections and fostering understanding in a world that is ever-changing and endlessly complex.

The Core Heart of Humans

Charles William Fortney from Petersburg Illinois USA Capella University Student Ambassador 4.0 GPA Information Technology with Multiple Media Specializations Musician Songwriter Performer CEO Wolf Sundown Entertainment Studios Father of 4 children and several grandchildren and Krystal Joy Smith a Nurse from Talula Illinois USA School of Nursing and "The Heart of Virtue" Award, have orchestrated a book for all humans for their hearts that you are sure to enjoy.

Reason

"The Heart of Humans" is a timeless and profound exploration that seeks to unravel the intricate mysteries of our existence, delving into the depths of the human heart to uncover the essence of our being. This book is a guiding light, illuminating the path towards self-discovery, personal growth, and interconnectedness.

At its core, "The Heart of Humans" invites readers to embark on a transformative journey of self-exploration and introspection. It encourages us to dive deep into the innermost chambers of our hearts, to discover the hidden treasures and truths that lie within. By embarking on this journey, we gain a deeper understanding of our passions, values, and purpose, unlocking the potential to live a life of meaning and fulfillment.

This book also delves into the power of belief and the impact it has on shaping our lives. It encourages us to nurture a sense of hope, faith, and optimism, recognizing the profound influence these qualities have on our personal growth and resilience. By cultivating a belief in ourselves and the possibilities that lie ahead, we can transcend limitations, overcome challenges, and create a life that aligns with our deepest desires.

Furthermore, "The Heart of Humans" explores the significance of the heart in our relationships and connections with others. It acknowledges that love, compassion, and empathy are the bonds that weave together the tapestry of human connection. By cultivating these qualities within ourselves, we foster meaningful relationships, build bridges of understanding, and create a sense of belonging and unity in our communities.

The book also delves into the ebbs and flows of life, recognizing that challenges and setbacks are an inherent part of the human experience. It emphasizes the importance of resilience and the power of the heart to guide us through difficult times. By tapping into our inner strength, we can navigate adversity, learn valuable lessons, and emerge stronger, wiser, and more compassionate.

Moreover, "The Heart of Humans" explores the interconnectedness of all living beings. It recognizes that we are part of a vast, intricate web of life, and our actions have ripple effects that extend far beyond ourselves. It emphasizes the significance of compassion, understanding, and empathy in creating a more harmonious and sustainable world. By embracing our interconnectedness, we can foster a sense of unity, promote social justice, and work towards a future that cherishes the well-being of all beings and the planet we call home.

"The Heart of Humans" is an invitation to embrace the unique journey each of us is on, to listen to the wisdom of our hearts, and to live authentically. It encourages us to cultivate a deep sense of self-awareness, to honor our passions, and to align our actions with our values. By doing so, we can create a life that is aligned with our true selves, filled with purpose, joy, and deep fulfillment.

In summary, "The Heart of Humans" is a transformative and expansive exploration into the depths of our existence. It serves as a guide, inspiring readers to embark on a journey of self-discovery, belief, and interconnectedness. Through its exploration of the human heart, this book offers profound insights, practical guidance, and timeless wisdom for living a life that is aligned with our truest selves and contributes to the well-being of all. It is a reminder that within each of us lies the power to shape our own destinies and create a world filled with love, understanding, and unity. The power in Prayer, hope and faith.

"The Core of the Heart" refers to its central and essential part. In the context of the text provided, "The Heart of Humans," the phrase "core of the heart" is used metaphorically to represent the central themes, messages, or essence of the human being. It signifies the fundamental aspects of life.

"Ten thousand angels could come down and it would make no difference."

Abraham Lincoln, New Salem Illinois USA is widely regarded as one of the greatest leaders in history, continues to inspire and captivate our imaginations with his profound words. Among his many timeless quotes, one that stands out is, "Ten thousand angels could come down and it would make no difference." This quote not only reveals Lincoln's deep understanding of the human condition, but it also invites us to contemplate the intricate relationship between divine intervention and human agency.

When Lincoln speaks of "ten thousand angels," he conjures up a vivid image of an overwhelming multitude of celestial beings, representing the epitome of divine intervention and supernatural forces. However, he poignantly suggests that even if such a vast number of heavenly beings were to descend upon the earth, their presence and intervention would have no discernible impact on the outcome or circumstances at hand. This thought-provoking statement compels us to ponder the intricate dynamics between external influences and the power of human choices.

By expressing this sentiment, Lincoln underscores his unwavering belief in the profound significance of human agency. He emphasizes that the ultimate power to shape our destinies resides within us, rather than relying solely on external forces or divine intervention. Lincoln's quote challenges us to recognize the immense potential we possess to effect change and to take responsibility for the choices and actions that shape our lives.

Furthermore, Lincoln's statement can be seen as a call to embrace self-reliance and personal accountability. He encourages individuals to cultivate their inner strength, determination, and resilience in the face of challenges. Rather than passively waiting for external assistance or divine intervention, Lincoln implores us to harness our own unique abilities and take decisive action to shape our own futures.

In addition to individual agency, Lincoln's quote carries a profound message about the transformative power of collective action. While the presence of ten thousand angels might initially evoke a sense of overwhelming force, Lincoln asserts that the impact of external intervention pales in comparison to the potential unleashed through united human effort. He suggests that true progress and transformation are most effectively achieved through collaboration and collective action, as individuals rally together towards a common purpose.

Moreover, Lincoln's quote invites us to reflect on the limitations of relying solely on external sources of support or intervention. While faith and spirituality can provide solace and guidance, he reminds us that true change ultimately emanates from within. It is through our own determination, resilience, and unwavering commitment to making a difference that we can bring about lasting and meaningful transformation.

In a broader context, Lincoln's quote speaks to the fundamental nature of the human experience. It serves as a timeless reminder that we possess inherent agency and the ability to shape our own lives, irrespective of external circumstances or supernatural forces. It is through our choices, actions, and values that we have the power to create a better world for ourselves and future generations.

In conclusion, Abraham Lincoln's quote, "Ten thousand angels could come down and it would make no difference," resonates as a profound testament to the immense impact of human agency and the remarkable potential that lies within collective action. It compels us to delve deep within ourselves, to summon our inner strength, and to recognize our shared responsibility in creating a more just, compassionate, and harmonious world. Lincoln's words inspire us to embrace our inherent power to effect change and to forge a path towards a brighter future, guided by our own choices and actions.

"The Core of the Heart" refers to its central and essential part. In the context of the text provided, "The Heart of Humans," the phrase "core of the heart" is used metaphorically to represent the central themes, messages, or essence of the human being. It signifies the fundamental aspects of life.

The Heart of Humans - Core of The Heart

The Heart of Humans "The Wizard of Oz" is a classic children's novel written by L. Frank Baum. The story follows a young girl named Dorothy who is swept away from her home in Kansas by a tornado and transported to the magical land of Oz. In her journey to find her way back home, Dorothy encounters various characters including the Scarecrow, the Tin Woodman, and the Cowardly Lion, who join her in her quest. Together, they travel to the Emerald City to seek help from the powerful Wizard of Oz. Along the way, they face challenges and overcome obstacles, learning important lessons about courage, friendship, and the importance of home. With the help of the Good Witch of the North, Dorothy eventually discovers that she has the power to return home all along, by clicking her heels three times and repeating, "There's no place like home." The story is a timeless tale of adventure, self-discovery, and the power of belief.

Self-discovery is a significant theme. Throughout the story, Dorothy embarks on a journey to find her way back home, but along the way, she comes to understand more about herself and her capabilities. As she faces challenges and overcomes obstacles, Dorothy learns to tap into her inner strength and resilience. She discovers that she possesses the power to return home all along, symbolized by the act of clicking her heels three times and repeating, "There's no place like home." This realization represents Dorothy's self-discovery, as she recognizes her own agency and the strength within herself to overcome adversity and achieve her goals. It is through her journey in the magical land of Oz that Dorothy learns to believe in herself and embrace her own power, ultimately leading to her self-discovery.

In "The Wizard of Oz," self-discovery is not only portrayed through Dorothy's physical journey to find her way back home but also through the metaphorical journey of the heart. As Dorothy faces challenges and overcomes obstacles in the magical land of Oz, she not only learns about her own capabilities but also discovers the power of love and compassion. Through her interactions with the Scarecrow, the Tinman, and the Cowardly Lion, Dorothy realizes that the true strength of the heart lies in kindness, empathy, and genuine connections with others. This realization leads to her self-discovery of the heart, as she understands the importance of nurturing and protecting the love within oneself and extending it to those around her.

The Wizard of Oz is a powerful figure in the story. He resides in the Emerald City and is believed to have the ability to grant the wishes of those who seek his help. Dorothy and her companions, the Scarecrow, the Tin Woodman, and the Cowardly Lion, travel to the Emerald City to seek the Wizard's assistance in finding their respective desires. However, it is later revealed that the Wizard is actually a normal man from Omaha, Nebraska, who arrived in Oz by accident. Despite not possessing magical powers, the Wizard uses his intelligence to fulfill the wishes of Dorothy and her friends. The Wizard of Oz represents the idea that true power lies within oneself and that individuals are capable of achieving their desires through their own abilities.

Jesus teaches us that man cannot live by bread and water alone. It emphasizes the importance of inner strength, self-belief, and the power within oneself to achieve desires and overcome challenges. The Wizard of Oz, despite not having magical powers, uses his intelligence and showmanship to fulfill the wishes of Dorothy and her friends, symbolizing the idea that true power lies within individuals and their own abilities. "The Oz" teaches us the significance of inner strength, self-belief, and the power within oneself to overcome challenges and achieve desires. Despite not having magical powers, the Wizard uses his intelligence and showmanship to fulfill the wishes of Dorothy and her friends, highlighting the idea that true power lies within individuals and their own abilities.

Changing our thoughts can have a profound impact on our feelings. We are able to overcome them by changing our thoughts and beliefs. Despite not having magical powers, the Wizard uses his intelligence and showmanship to fulfill the wishes of Dorothy and her friends. This highlights the idea that by changing our thoughts and believing in our own abilities, we can harness our inner strength and achieve our goals. It teaches us that true power comes from within ourselves and that we have the capability to transform our feelings by changing our thoughts.

"The great spirit highlights the belief that individuals have the capability to harness their inner strength and achieve their goals. Faith without work is dead. This concept emphasizes that simply having faith or belief in something is not enough; it must be accompanied by action and effort in order to be meaningful and effective.

In many aspects of life, including personal growth, relationships, and professional success, faith without work is indeed dead. It is through our actions and the work we put into our endeavors that we can bring our visions and aspirations to life. Without taking the necessary steps and putting in the required effort, our faith remains stagnant and lacks the power to create tangible results.

Consider a person who has a dream of starting their own business. They may have unwavering faith in their abilities and the potential success of their business idea. However, if they do not take the necessary steps to research, plan, and execute their business plan, their faith alone will not lead to actualizing their dream. It is the combination of their belief and the work they put into developing the business that brings it to fruition.

Similarly, in personal growth and self-improvement, having faith in our potential to change and grow is crucial. But without taking action and putting in the work to develop new skills, break old habits, or pursue opportunities for growth, our faith in ourselves will remain stagnant. It is through the consistent effort and dedication to our personal development that we can truly unleash our inner strength and achieve our goals.

In relationships, faith without work can also lead to stagnation or deterioration. While trust and belief in the strength of a relationship are important, they must be accompanied by active effort and commitment. Without investing time, energy, and care into nurturing and maintaining the relationship, faith alone will not sustain it. It is through the consistent work of communication, compromise, and emotional support that relationships can thrive and grow.

In summary, the belief that faith without work is dead serves as a reminder that action and effort are essential for bringing about desired outcomes. It encourages individuals to combine their faith and belief with tangible steps and hard work to achieve their goals. Whether in personal growth, relationships, or pursuing professional aspirations, it is through the combination of faith and work that we can truly harness our inner strength and create meaningful and lasting change in our lives. It teaches us that true power resides within ourselves and can be accessed by changing our thoughts and beliefs. I myself am a self-help author and motivational speaker who emphasized the power of positive thinking and belief in oneself. I believe that our thoughts shape our reality and that by changing our thoughts, we can change our lives. True power comes from within ourselves, and we have the ability to tap into our inner strength and achieve our goals. My teachings align with the message which emphasizes the idea that true power resides within oneself and can be accessed by changing our thoughts and beliefs. The Wizard of Oz, Dr. Wayne Dyer and Jesus do emphasize the power of thoughts and beliefs. They highlight that our thoughts shape our reality and that by changing our thoughts, we can change our lives. They suggest that true power comes from within, and we have the ability to tap into our inner strength and achieve our goals by harnessing the power of our thoughts. Jesus stated, "If you've done it in your mind, you have done it".

This message can be seen as positive and empowering, as it encourages individuals to take control of their thoughts and beliefs in order to create positive change in their lives. By recognizing that our thoughts have the power to shape our reality, we can cultivate a positive mindset and focus on achieving our goals.

On the other hand, some may argue that this message can be misleading or oversimplified. While thoughts and beliefs are important, they alone may not guarantee success or overcoming all obstacles. External factors and circumstances can also play a significant role in shaping outcomes. It is important to acknowledge the complexities of life and to consider a holistic approach that combines positive thinking with practical actions and perseverance.

The emphasis on the power of thoughts and beliefs can be seen as both empowering and potentially oversimplified. While the notion of the soul is not directly addressed, it is implied that good and bad desires are inherent in human consciousness. The story highlights the importance of positive qualities like kindness, empathy, and genuine connections with others, which are portrayed as essential for personal growth and self-discovery.

The concept of good and bad desires is implied but not explicitly discussed. However, it is important to highlight the significance of positive qualities such as kindness, empathy, and genuine connections with others. These qualities are portrayed as essential for personal growth and self-discovery. The text suggests that nurturing and protecting the love within oneself and extending it to others is a positive desire, while selfishness and harmful intentions are considered negative desires.

Moreover, it is worth noting the emphasis placed on the power of positive qualities and actions. The text encourages individuals to actively cultivate good desires and strive for personal growth. It also emphasizes the importance of fostering meaningful connections with others, as these connections can greatly contribute to one's overall well-being and fulfillment.

God

"God" varies across different religious, spiritual, and cultural beliefs. In general terms, "God" is often understood as a supreme being or higher power that is believed to have created and governs the universe.

The specific characteristics and attributes attributed to God can vary greatly depending on individual beliefs and religious traditions. Some view God as a personal and loving deity, while others see God as an impersonal force or energy.

Additionally, different religions and belief systems have their own interpretations of God, with varying names, forms, and teachings. For example, in Christianity, God is often described as the Holy Trinity consisting of the Father, Son (Jesus Christ), and the Holy Spirit. In Islam, God is referred to as Allah and is believed to be singular, all-powerful, and merciful.

It is important to note that discussions about God are deeply rooted in faith, spirituality, and personal beliefs. The understanding and interpretation of God can differ significantly among individuals and communities, and it is a topic that has been debated and explored by theologians, philosophers, and scholars throughout history.

The role of God and what He does for humans varies among different religious beliefs and interpretations. In general, God is believed to have created the universe and everything within it, including humans. Many religious traditions teach that God provides guidance, love, and forgiveness to humans. He is seen as a source of strength, comfort, and hope. Additionally, some believe that God plays a role in shaping human destinies and offers salvation or eternal life. It is important to note that the specifics of what God does for humans can differ based on individual beliefs and religious doctrines.

Angels are celestial beings that hold significant roles in various religious and spiritual traditions. Often depicted as benevolent messengers of God, angels are believed to serve as intermediaries between the divine and humanity. Throughout history, angels have been associated with a range of qualities and attributes, including protection, guidance, and divine intervention.

In many religious traditions, angels are seen as celestial beings created by God to carry out His will and assist humans in their spiritual journeys. They are believed to possess immense knowledge and wisdom, acting as conduits of divine messages and guidance. Angels are often depicted as beings of pure light and beauty, radiating a sense of peace and tranquility.

One of the primary roles of angels is to provide protection and watch over individuals. They are believed to act as guardians, shielding humans from harm and evil influences. Angels are seen as spiritual warriors, fighting against darkness and negative forces to ensure the safety and well-being of those under their care. Many individuals find comfort and solace in the belief that they are constantly surrounded by angelic presence and protection.

Furthermore, angels are believed to offer guidance and support to humans in times of need. They are seen as compassionate beings who offer comfort and reassurance during difficult or challenging situations. Angels are thought to provide inspiration and insight, helping individuals find their true purpose and navigate the complexities of life. Many people turn to angels in times of uncertainty or when seeking guidance on important decisions.

Divine intervention is another aspect often associated with angels. They are believed to have the ability to intervene in human affairs, bringing about miraculous events or unexpected outcomes. Angels are seen as conduits of God's power and mercy, capable of performing acts that transcend the natural order of things. Stories and accounts of angelic interventions can be found in religious texts and personal testimonies, reinforcing the belief in their extraordinary abilities.

It is important to note that the understanding and interpretation of angels can vary among different religious and spiritual traditions.

The specifics of their nature, hierarchy, and roles may differ, but the underlying belief in their existence and their connection to the divine remains a common thread.

In summary, angels are celestial beings revered in various religious and spiritual traditions. They are believed to serve as messengers of God, offering protection, guidance, and divine intervention to humans. Angels are seen as benevolent beings of light and beauty, acting as intermediaries between the divine and humanity. Their roles and attributes may vary, but their presence and influence are widely recognized and celebrated.

Prayer is a profound and sacred practice that holds great significance in various religious and spiritual traditions. It is a form of communication with the divine, a way for individuals to connect with and express their reverence, gratitude, supplication, or worship to a higher power. Through prayer, individuals seek solace, guidance, strength, and a deeper connection with the divine and angelic beings.

Prayer takes on many forms and can vary greatly depending on cultural, theological, and personal beliefs. It can be a silent contemplation, a heartfelt conversation, a recitation of sacred texts, or a communal ritual. Regardless of the specific method, prayer is a deeply personal and intimate experience that allows individuals to express their innermost thoughts, feelings, and desires to the divine.

In the context of angels, prayer takes on a special significance. Angels are believed to be celestial beings created by God to serve as messengers and intermediaries between the divine and humanity. They are seen as benevolent beings of light and beauty, radiating a sense of peace and tranquility. Many individuals turn to prayer as a means of connecting with angels and seeking their guidance, protection, and intervention. Through prayer, individuals express their trust, faith, and belief in the presence and power of angels in their lives.

Prayer to angels can encompass a wide range of intentions and requests. Some may pray to angels for protection, asking for their watchful presence and guidance in times of danger or uncertainty. Others may seek angelic assistance in matters of health, relationships, or personal challenges, asking for healing, comfort, or resolution. Prayer to angels can also involve seeking spiritual guidance and wisdom, asking for insight and clarity in navigating life's complexities. Additionally, individuals may offer prayers of gratitude and thanksgiving, acknowledging the blessings and support they have received from angelic beings.

The act of prayer itself is transformative and can have a profound impact on individuals. It allows for a deepening of one's spiritual connection, fostering a sense of peace, solace, and inner strength. Prayer provides a space for reflection, self-discovery, and the cultivation of a personal relationship with the divine. It can bring comfort and reassurance, offering a sense of being heard and understood by the divine and angelic beings.

It is important to recognize that the understanding and interpretation of prayer can vary among different religious and spiritual traditions. Each tradition may have its own specific rituals, prayers, and beliefs surrounding the practice. Some may emphasize specific prayers or invocations to particular angels, while others may have a more general approach. Regardless of the specific practices, prayer remains a universal and powerful means of connecting with the divine and seeking the assistance and presence of angels.

In conclusion, prayer is a deeply meaningful and transformative practice that allows individuals to connect with the divine and seek the guidance, protection, and intervention of angelic beings. It is a personal and intimate expression of reverence, gratitude, supplication, or worship, reflecting one's beliefs, desires, and relationship with the divine. Through prayer, individuals can find solace, strength, and a deepening of their spiritual connection, knowing that they are heard and supported by the angels in their journey.

Devine guidance

Divine guidance is a profound and transformative concept that encompasses the belief that individuals can receive spiritual direction, wisdom, and support from a higher power or divine beings. It is a deeply personal and intimate connection with the divine that allows individuals to seek guidance and assistance in their lives.

The belief in divine guidance is rooted in the understanding that there is a greater intelligence at work in the universe, beyond what can be comprehended by human reasoning alone. It is the recognition that there is a divine order and purpose to life, and that by aligning oneself with this higher power, individuals can tap into a wellspring of wisdom and guidance.

One of the primary ways individuals seek divine guidance is through prayer. Prayer is a sacred practice that allows individuals to communicate with the divine and express their desires, concerns, gratitude, and intentions. It is a means of opening oneself up to receive divine insights and messages, and to seek clarity and direction in various aspects of life.

In addition to prayer, individuals may also seek divine guidance through meditation, contemplation, or other spiritual practices. These practices create a space for individuals to quiet the mind, connect with their inner selves, and open up to the presence of the divine. Through these practices, individuals can cultivate a heightened state of awareness and receptivity, enabling them to receive guidance and insights from the divine.

Divine guidance can manifest in various ways. It may come in the form of intuitive insights, where individuals receive a deep knowing or understanding about a particular situation or decision. It may also come through signs and synchronicities, where individuals notice meaningful coincidences or symbols that serve as messages from the divine. Additionally, divine guidance can be felt as a gentle nudging or inner prompting, guiding individuals towards certain actions or choices.

The experience of divine guidance can be deeply transformative and empowering. It provides individuals with a sense of support and reassurance, knowing that they are not alone in their journey. It offers clarity and direction, helping individuals make decisions, navigate challenges, and find a sense of purpose and fulfillment. Divine guidance can also bring a profound sense of peace and alignment, as individuals trust in the wisdom and benevolence of the divine.

It is important to note that the experience of divine guidance is highly personal and subjective. It may vary greatly among individuals based on their beliefs, spiritual practices, and openness to receiving guidance. What may be perceived as divine guidance for one person may be different for another. It is a deeply individual and unique experience that is shaped by each person's relationship with the divine.

In conclusion, divine guidance is a profound and transformative concept that encompasses the belief that individuals can receive spiritual direction, wisdom, and support from a higher power or divine beings. It is a deeply personal and intimate connection with the divine that allows individuals to seek guidance, clarity, and purpose in their lives. Through prayer, meditation, and other spiritual practices, individuals can open themselves up to receive divine insights, signs, and inner promptings. The experience of divine guidance is highly personal and subjective, providing individuals with a sense of support, empowerment, and alignment with the divine.

The concept of the greater god ethics of humans is a profound and multifaceted topic that has been explored and debated throughout history. It encompasses the belief that ethical principles and values are derived from a higher power or divine source, shaping the moral compass of individuals and guiding human behavior.

Ethics, in general, refer to the study of moral principles and values that govern human conduct. They provide a framework for individuals to determine what is right or wrong, just or unjust, and guide their actions accordingly. The belief in a greater god ethics adds a spiritual dimension to this framework, suggesting that ethical principles are not solely derived from human reasoning or societal norms, but are rooted in a transcendent source of moral guidance.

Many religious and spiritual traditions teach that humans have a moral responsibility to live by certain ethical principles and values, which are believed to be bestowed upon them by a higher power or divine beings. These ethical principles often revolve around concepts such as love, compassion, honesty, fairness, and respect for others. They provide a moral compass that influences human behavior and fosters a sense of interconnectedness and responsibility towards fellow beings and the world at large.

The belief in a greater god ethics underscores the idea that ethical behavior is not solely based on personal preferences or societal norms, but is rooted in a higher, transcendent source of moral guidance. It suggests that ethical principles are not arbitrary human constructs but are derived from a divine wisdom that surpasses human understanding. This belief adds a sense of sacredness and accountability to ethical decision-making, as individuals strive to align their actions with the will of the divine.

The greater god ethics of humans play a significant role in shaping individual and collective behavior. They provide a moral framework that guides individuals in making decisions and interacting with others. These ethical principles emphasize the importance of treating others with kindness, fairness, and respect, and promote the well-being and flourishing of all individuals. They encourage individuals to act in ways that are aligned with the greater good and to consider the broader impact of their actions on society and the environment.

Furthermore, the belief in a greater god ethics fosters a sense of moral duty and responsibility. It reminds individuals that their actions have consequences not only in the present but also in the spiritual realm. This belief encourages individuals to strive for moral excellence, seeking to embody the virtues and values that are believed to be pleasing to the divine.

It is important to note that ethical frameworks and beliefs can differ among different religious and philosophical traditions. The specifics of the greater god ethics and their application to human behavior may vary based on individual interpretations and cultural contexts. Additionally, ethical considerations can also be influenced by societal norms, personal values, and the complexities of human experience.

In summary, the greater god ethics of humans reflects the belief that ethical principles and values are derived from a higher power or divine source. They provide a moral compass that guides human behavior and fosters a sense of interconnectedness and responsibility towards others. The belief in a greater god ethics adds a spiritual dimension to ethical decision-making, acknowledging the transcendent source of moral guidance. These ethics emphasize concepts such as love, compassion, fairness, and respect, and encourage individuals to align their actions with the greater good. The belief in a greater god ethics adds a sense of sacredness and accountability to ethical behavior, reminding individuals of their moral duty and responsibility in the spiritual realm.

A moral compass is a fundamental aspect of human existence that plays a significant role in guiding individuals' actions, shaping their character, and influencing their interactions with others. It serves as a compass, providing individuals with a sense of direction and guiding them towards ethical behavior and decision-making.

One of the key reasons for having a moral compass is to navigate the complexities of right and wrong in various situations. Ethics, the study of moral principles and values, provides a framework for individuals to determine what is morally acceptable or unacceptable. A moral compass acts as a personal GPS, helping individuals navigate through the moral landscape by providing them with a clear sense of what is right and wrong based on their values and beliefs.

Having a moral compass also promotes consistency and integrity in one's actions. It ensures that individuals act in a manner that is consistent with their values, regardless of external pressures or circumstances. A strong moral compass acts as a moral anchor, helping individuals stay true to their principles and maintain their integrity even when faced with difficult choices or temptations. This consistency in behavior contributes to the development of a strong moral character and fosters trust and respect from others.

Moreover, a moral compass fosters a sense of accountability and responsibility. It reminds individuals of their duty towards others and encourages them to consider the consequences of their actions on the well-being and rights of others. A moral compass promotes empathy, fairness, and respect for others, guiding individuals towards choices that promote the greater good and contribute positively to society. By aligning their actions with their moral compass, individuals take responsibility for their behavior and acknowledge their role in creating a just and compassionate world.

Furthermore, a moral compass provides individuals with a sense of purpose and meaning in their lives. It helps individuals define their values and principles, guiding them in leading a life that is aligned with their personal beliefs and aspirations. By following their moral compass, individuals can find fulfillment and satisfaction in knowing that their actions are consistent with their deeply held beliefs and values. This sense of purpose and meaning enhances their overall well-being and contributes to their personal growth and development.

Additionally, a moral compass serves as a source of guidance during times of uncertainty or moral dilemmas. It provides individuals with a framework to evaluate their options and make informed decisions that are in line with their ethical values. A moral compass helps individuals navigate through complex ethical situations by considering the consequences of their actions, the impact on others, and the principles that guide their behavior. It empowers individuals to make choices that they can be proud of and that contribute to their personal growth and the betterment of society.

In conclusion, a moral compass is an essential tool that guides individuals in making ethical decisions and shaping their behavior. It provides a sense of direction, consistency, integrity, accountability, and purpose in navigating the complexities of right and wrong. By following their moral compass, individuals can lead a more ethical, meaningful, and fulfilling life, making choices that align with their values and contribute positively to the world around them.

"Mastering by always learning" is a transformative philosophy that emphasizes the continuous pursuit of knowledge, growth, and improvement as a means to achieve true mastery in any area of life. It recognizes that mastery is not a destination to be reached, but rather an ongoing journey of self-discovery, skill development, and personal evolution.

At the heart of this philosophy is the understanding that learning is a lifelong endeavor. It is not confined to a specific time or place but is a constant process that permeates every aspect of our lives. Whether it is acquiring new skills, expanding our knowledge, or deepening our understanding of ourselves and the world around us, learning provides the essential foundation for growth and mastery.

The path to mastery begins with a humble recognition of our own limitations and a commitment to continuous improvement. It requires a growth mindset, where we believe that our abilities and talents can be developed through dedication, effort, and the willingness to learn from both successes and failures. By embracing a mindset of continuous learning, we open ourselves up to new possibilities, expand our horizons, and unlock our full potential.

Learning is not limited to formal education or structured environments. It can take many forms, such as reading books, attending seminars, seeking mentorship, engaging in hands-on experiences, and reflecting on our own experiences. Every encounter, whether big or small, presents an opportunity for learning and growth. By approaching life with a thirst for knowledge and a curiosity to explore new ideas, we cultivate a mindset of continuous learning that propels us towards mastery.

The pursuit of mastery requires discipline, perseverance, and a willingness to step outside of our comfort zones. It involves setting goals, developing a plan of action, and consistently putting in the effort to improve. Along the way, we may encounter challenges and setbacks, but it is through these experiences that we gain valuable insights, build resilience, and develop the skills necessary to overcome obstacles.

Furthermore, the journey towards mastery is not just about acquiring technical skills and expertise. It also involves personal growth, emotional intelligence, and a deep understanding of ourselves. By learning about our strengths, weaknesses, values, and passions, we can align our actions and choices with our authentic selves, leading to a more fulfilling and purposeful life.

The pursuit of mastery is a deeply rewarding and fulfilling endeavor. As we progress on this journey, we experience a sense of accomplishment and satisfaction in our growth and progress. However, true mastery is not characterized by a sense of arrival or completion. It is an ongoing process of refinement and self-improvement, where there is always room for growth and further exploration.

Moreover, the journey towards mastery is not a solitary one. It is enriched by the connections and collaborations we form with others along the way. Engaging in meaningful interactions, seeking out diverse perspectives, and learning from the experiences of others can enhance our own learning and accelerate our progress towards mastery.

In addition, the pursuit of mastery extends beyond the boundaries of a specific domain or discipline. It encompasses a holistic approach to personal and professional development. It involves cultivating a growth mindset, nurturing our mental and emotional well-being, and embracing lifelong learning as a way of life. By integrating different areas of knowledge and skills, we can achieve a multidimensional mastery that transcends traditional boundaries.

Furthermore, the journey towards mastery is not limited to just one area of life. It can be applied to various aspects, such as career, relationships, personal development, creative pursuits, and even our impact on society. By adopting the mindset of mastering by always learning, we approach each area with curiosity, dedication, and a commitment to growth, allowing us to continuously evolve and excel in every facet of our lives.

In conclusion, "mastering by always learning" is a transformative philosophy that encourages us to embrace a mindset of continuous growth, improvement, and self-discovery. It reminds us that mastery is not a destination but a lifelong journey of learning, skill development, and personal evolution. By committing ourselves to the pursuit of knowledge, embracing challenges as opportunities for growth, cultivating self-awareness, engaging with others, adopting a holistic approach, and applying this philosophy to various aspects of life, we can embark on a path that leads to true mastery in every area of our lives. Let us embrace the joy of learning and the pursuit of mastery, for it is in this lifelong journey that we find the fulfillment, purpose, and endless possibilities we seek.

Hardening the Heart

Hardening the heart by suppressing the soul through negative thoughts can have detrimental effects on one's spiritual well-being. When we close ourselves off to our true emotions and suppress our innermost desires, we limit our ability to connect with our higher self and the divine guidance that is available to us. Instead of allowing our hearts to remain open and receptive, we block the flow of love, compassion, and spiritual growth.

By hardening the heart through negative thoughts and suppressing the soul, we cut ourselves off from the wisdom and guidance that the divine offers us. It is important to recognize that true strength and resilience come from embracing our emotions, acknowledging our vulnerabilities, and allowing ourselves to experience the full range of human experiences. By doing so, we create space for growth, healing, and connection with our higher selves and the divine.

Instead of hardening our hearts and suppressing our souls, let us strive to cultivate a mindset of openness, compassion, and self-acceptance. By embracing our emotions and allowing ourselves to be vulnerable, we invite the divine guidance and support that can help us navigate life's challenges with grace and wisdom. Let us choose to nurture our souls and keep our hearts open, for it is through this openness that we can experience true spiritual growth and fulfillment.

In a world often plagued by revenge and hate, it is imperative for us to rise above these destructive forces and embrace a higher level of consciousness, compassion, and understanding. Rather than succumbing to the vicious cycle of seeking revenge or allowing hate to consume our hearts, let us choose a path that is rooted in healing, forgiveness, and love. By doing so, we can contribute to the transformation of ourselves and the world around us.

Revenge, driven by anger and resentment, only perpetuates a cycle of pain and suffering. It blinds us from the potential for growth and healing, trapping us in a never-ending loop of negativity. However, by consciously choosing forgiveness, we break free from this cycle and create an opportunity for profound personal and spiritual growth.

Forgiveness is not a sign of weakness or a justification of the actions that have caused us harm. On the contrary, it is an act of strength, liberation, and reclaiming our own power. When we choose forgiveness, we release the heavy burden of negative emotions and create space within ourselves for healing, peace, and happiness. It is an act of self-empowerment that enables us to take control of our own lives and define our own narrative, rather than being defined by the actions of others.

Forgiveness is a deeply personal and transformative journey. It requires introspection, self-reflection, and the willingness to extend empathy and understanding towards those who have wronged us. It may involve confronting our own pain, acknowledging our vulnerabilities, and finding the strength to let go of resentment. Through this journey, we learn valuable lessons about ourselves, our values, and the power of compassion.

In choosing forgiveness, we also open ourselves up to the transformative power of love and understanding. Love is the antidote to hate, and by replacing hatred with compassion, we foster an environment of healing and growth. Love has the ability to bridge divides, mend broken relationships, and cultivate unity. When we choose love over hate, we contribute to the collective well-being and create a harmonious space for everyone to thrive.

Nurturing our souls and keeping our hearts open is an ongoing practice that requires dedication and self-care. It involves cultivating a mindset of empathy, compassion, and self-acceptance. By embracing our emotions and allowing ourselves to be vulnerable, we invite divine guidance and support into our lives. This openness allows us to navigate life's challenges with grace, wisdom, and resilience. It is through this openness that we can experience true spiritual growth, personal fulfillment, and a deep connection with ourselves and the world around us.

In a world that often glorifies revenge and holds onto grudges, choosing forgiveness and love requires immense courage and strength. It is a conscious decision to rise above negativity, to let go of the past, and to create a ripple effect of positivity and healing. By choosing forgiveness, we not only liberate ourselves from the shackles of hate but also inspire others to embark on their own journey of forgiveness and transformation.

Let us remember that forgiveness is a journey, and it is okay to take our time. It is a deeply personal process, and everyone's path may look different. Along this journey, it is important to seek support from trusted friends, family, or professionals who can provide guidance, encouragement, and a safe space for healing.

Together, let us commit to being agents of change and spreading love and understanding wherever we go. By choosing forgiveness over revenge and hate, we contribute to the creation of a more compassionate and harmonious world. Each act of forgiveness, no matter how small, has the power to create a profound impact on our own lives and the lives of those around us.

So, let us embrace the transformative power of forgiveness and love. Let us commit to nurturing our souls, keeping our hearts open, and actively choosing compassion and understanding even in the face of adversity. By doing so, we become catalysts for positive change and help create a world that is built on empathy, forgiveness, and true spiritual growth.

True happiness can indeed be found in contentment. Contentment is the state of being satisfied and at peace with what one has, without constantly desiring more or comparing oneself to others. It is a deep sense of inner fulfillment and gratitude that transcends external circumstances.

In a world that often equates happiness with material possessions, achievements, or external validation, contentment offers a different perspective. It reminds us that true happiness does not come from accumulating more things or reaching a certain level of success, but rather from cultivating a sense of inner peace and appreciation for the present moment.

Contentment allows us to find joy in the simple pleasures of life - a warm cup of tea, a beautiful sunset, or the laughter of loved ones. It shifts our focus from constantly striving for more to appreciating and embracing the abundance that already exists in our lives. It is about finding contentment in the ordinary and recognizing the extraordinary within it.

Moreover, contentment frees us from the cycle of comparison and envy. When we are content with ourselves and our circumstances, we are less likely to feel the need to measure our worth against others or constantly seek external validation. Instead, we can embrace our unique journey and celebrate the achievements and successes of others without feeling threatened or inadequate.

Contentment is not about settling for less or becoming complacent. It is about finding a balance between ambition and acceptance. It is about setting realistic goals and working towards them, while also recognizing and appreciating the progress we have already made. Contentment allows us to strive for growth and improvement while maintaining a sense of peace and fulfillment in the present.

By cultivating contentment, we can experience a deeper sense of well-being and happiness. We become less dependent on external circumstances or achievements for our happiness, and instead, find joy in the present moment and in the relationships and experiences that truly matter. Contentment allows us to savor the journey rather than constantly chasing after the destination.

However, it is important to note that contentment does not mean we should stop striving for personal growth or pursuing our dreams. It simply means that we can find happiness and fulfillment along the way, rather than postponing our happiness until we achieve certain goals or acquire specific things. Contentment allows us to appreciate both the process and the outcome, finding joy and satisfaction in our efforts and progress.

In a society that often promotes an insatiable desire for more, contentment offers a counterbalance. It encourages us to pause, reflect, and appreciate the blessings in our lives. It reminds us to be mindful of the present moment and to cultivate a deep sense of gratitude for what we have.

Contentment also plays a crucial role in our mental and emotional well-being. When we are content, we experience less stress, anxiety, and discontent. We are able to navigate life's challenges with greater resilience and perspective. Contentment allows us to let go of the constant need for external validation and instead focus on nurturing our inner selves.

Moreover, contentment fosters healthy relationships. When we are content within ourselves, we are more likely to cultivate healthy and fulfilling connections with others. Contentment allows us to be fully present in our relationships, to appreciate and accept others as they are, and to foster a sense of deep connection and understanding.

In a fast-paced and consumer-driven culture, cultivating contentment can be a radical act of self-care and resistance. It challenges the notion that our worth is determined by external factors and invites us to redefine success and happiness on our own terms. Contentment empowers us to take control of our own well-being and to create a life that is aligned with our values and true desires.

Ultimately, true happiness is a deeply personal and subjective experience. While contentment can certainly contribute to our overall sense of well-being, each individual may have their own unique path to happiness. It is important to honor and respect our own journey, while also embracing the wisdom that contentment can bring.

So, let us cultivate contentment in our lives. Let us find joy in the present moment and appreciate the abundance that already surrounds us. By embracing contentment, we can experience true happiness and live a life filled with gratitude, peace, and fulfillment. May we find contentment in the journey of life and allow it to guide us towards a deeper sense of happiness and fulfillment.

Nature of life

The nature of life is a profound and awe-inspiring phenomenon that has captivated the curiosity and imagination of humanity since the dawn of civilization. It encompasses a vast array of interconnected processes, intricate mechanisms, and intrinsic qualities that define the existence and essence of living organisms, forming the very fabric of our world.

At its core, life is characterized by an astonishing level of complexity and organization that sets it apart from the inanimate matter surrounding us. It is the symphony of cells, the building blocks of life, working in harmony to carry out the countless functions necessary for the sustenance and perpetuation of life. Within these cells, a symphony of biochemical reactions and molecular interactions take place, orchestrated with microscopic precision, enabling the maintenance of homeostasis, the production of energy, and the execution of countless biological processes that are the very essence of life.

Reproduction stands as a fundamental aspect of life, serving as the bridge between generations and ensuring the continuity and perpetuation of species. Through a remarkable array of reproductive strategies, from the intricate dance of sexual reproduction to the efficient simplicity of asexual reproduction, organisms possess the capacity to generate offspring that inherit their genetic information, passing on the blueprint of life itself. This diversity in reproductive mechanisms contributes to the incredible richness and variety of life forms that populate our planet, each with its own unique adaptations and characteristics.

Growth is an inherent characteristic of life that allows organisms to undergo physical and developmental changes, leading to an increase in size, complexity, and functionality. From the moment of conception, living organisms embark on a journey of growth, guided by intricate genetic programs and influenced by environmental factors. This continuous process of growth enables organisms to adapt to their surroundings, acquire resources, and fulfill their biological functions, laying the foundation for survival and reproduction.

Living organisms possess the extraordinary ability to respond to stimuli from their environment, displaying an intricate web of interactions between themselves and the world around them. Sensing and perceiving the world through specialized structures and sensory organs, organisms are equipped with intricate signaling pathways that allow them to detect and interpret external or internal cues. This responsiveness enables organisms to navigate their environment, avoid threats, seek resources, and engage in complex behaviors necessary for survival and reproduction. It is through this dynamic and responsive nature that organisms interact with the ecosystem, contributing to the delicate balance of life on Earth.

Life thrives in a magnificent tapestry of diversity, encompassing an astonishing range of species, ecosystems, and ecological interactions. From the microscopic world of bacteria and fungi to the grandeur of forests, oceans, and savannahs, the biosphere is a testament to the adaptability, resilience, and creativity of life. Each organism is uniquely adapted to its ecological niche, displaying an array of physiological, anatomical, and behavioral adaptations that enable it to survive and flourish. The interconnectedness of these diverse life forms intricate ecological networks, where every species plays a vital role in the functioning and stability of the ecosystem.

The nature of life has been the subject of profound inquiry, exploration, and contemplation across various disciplines. Scientists delve into the origins of life, investigating the conditions and processes that gave rise to the first living organisms on Earth. They study the mechanisms of evolution, uncovering the intricate patterns of genetic variation and selection that have shaped the diversity of life we observe today. Philosophers ponder the nature of consciousness, the meaning of life, and the ethical implications of our interactions with other living beings. Artists and poets seek to capture the essence and beauty of life, using their creative expression to evoke awe and wonder in others.

Understanding the nature of life provides us with a profound appreciation for the interconnectedness and interdependence of all living things. It reminds us of our place in the web of life and our shared responsibility as caretakers of the planet. It invites us to marvel at the beauty and complexity of the natural world, nurturing a sense of wonder and reverence for the miracle of life in all its forms.

In conclusion, the nature of life encompasses the intricate and interconnected processes, mechanisms, and qualities that define living organisms. It encompasses the complexity and organization of cells, the capacity for reproduction and growth, the responsiveness to stimuli, and the astonishing diversity of life forms. Exploring the nature of life expands our understanding of the world, deepens our connection with the natural environment, and ignites a sense of awe, wonder, and reverence for the wonders of existence that surround us every day.

Empathy

Empathy is a fundamental aspect of human nature that plays a vital role in our interactions, relationships, and overall well-being. It is the ability to understand and share the feelings, emotions, and experiences of others, putting ourselves in their shoes and offering support and compassion.

In "The Wizard of Oz," empathy is a significant theme that is exemplified through the actions and behaviors of the characters. Dorothy, the Scarecrow, the Tinman, and the Cowardly Lion all demonstrate empathy towards one another and the various characters they encounter in the magical land of Oz.

Dorothy, the protagonist of the story, displays empathy from the very beginning. When she first arrives in Oz, she sympathizes with the Munchkins who are being oppressed by the Wicked Witch of the East. She shows understanding and compassion towards their plight, and her empathy motivates her to embark on a journey to seek help from the Wizard of Oz.

Throughout their journey, Dorothy and her companions encounter a variety of characters, each with their own struggles and challenges. In each interaction, they demonstrate empathy by actively listening, offering support, and providing a helping hand. Whether it is the Scarecrow comforting the Crow who has lost his nest, the Tinman helping the Winkie who is trapped under a tree, or the Cowardly Lion offering encouragement to the Hungry Tiger, their empathy shines through in their actions.

The Scarecrow, despite being made of straw and supposedly lacking a brain, exhibits a remarkable level of empathy. He constantly supports and encourages Dorothy, the Tinman, and the Cowardly Lion throughout their journey. He listens attentively to their concerns and offers comforting words, showing a deep understanding of their emotions and demonstrating his empathy towards their struggles.

The Tinman, who desires a heart, is a symbol of empathy himself. Despite his seemingly rigid exterior, he has a compassionate and caring nature. He is quick to offer assistance and comfort to those in need, whether it is the animals in the enchanted forest or his companions who face their own challenges. His empathy is evident in his willingness to prioritize the well-being of others and to form deep emotional connections.

The Cowardly Lion, initially portrayed as fearful and lacking courage, discovers his own capacity for empathy as the story progresses. He supports his friends and shows understanding towards their fears and insecurities. His empathy enables him to confront his own fears and find the courage within himself to face the challenges they encounter on their quest.

Together, Dorothy and her companions exemplify the transformative power of empathy. Through their empathy, they form genuine connections with one another and the characters they meet along the way. They offer support, understanding, and kindness, creating a sense of unity and companionship that helps them overcome obstacles and ultimately find their respective desires.

"The Wizard of Oz" emphasizes the importance of empathy in fostering positive relationships and personal growth. It reminds us of the profound impact that empathy can have on our lives and the lives of others. By practicing empathy, we can create a more compassionate and understanding world, where individuals feel seen, heard, and validated.

In our own lives, empathy allows us to forge deeper connections with others, to navigate conflicts with understanding, and to offer support and comfort when needed. It helps us to develop a greater appreciation for the diversity of human experiences and perspectives, fostering a sense of unity and empathy towards people from different backgrounds and cultures.

Moreover, empathy has a profound impact on our own well-being. When we practice empathy, we cultivate a greater sense of emotional intelligence and self-awareness. We become more attuned to our own emotions and those of others, enhancing our ability to navigate social interactions and build meaningful relationships.

Furthermore, empathy plays a crucial role in promoting social justice and equality. It allows us to recognize and challenge our own biases and prejudices, opening our minds to different perspectives and experiences. By empathizing with others, we can work towards dismantling systemic barriers and creating a more inclusive and equitable society.

In conclusion, empathy is a powerful and transformative quality that is exemplified in "The Wizard of Oz." The characters in the story demonstrate empathy towards one another and the individuals they encounter, highlighting the importance of understanding, compassion, and support. By embracing empathy in our own lives, we can foster positive relationships, promote personal growth, contribute to social justice, and create a more compassionate and empathetic world. Through empathy, we can truly make a difference in the lives of others and in the world we inhabit.

"The Heart of Humans" is a captivating and thought-provoking book created by CW Fortney. It delves deep into the essence of human nature, exploring the themes of self-discovery, belief, and the power of the human heart. The story follows the journey of Dorothy, a young and curious girl who finds herself transported to the enchanting land of Oz. As Dorothy embarks on a quest to find her way back home, she encounters a host of fascinating characters and experiences that shape her understanding of herself and the world around her.

Throughout her adventure, Dorothy learns valuable lessons about courage, friendship, and the importance of belonging. She discovers that true power resides within oneself, and that by changing our thoughts and beliefs, we can unlock our potential and shape our own destiny. "The Heart of Humans" emphasizes the transformative power of positive qualities such as kindness, empathy, and genuine connections with others.

One of the central themes in the book is the idea that our beliefs and perceptions shape our reality. Dorothy learns that by shifting her mindset and embracing a belief in herself, she is able to overcome obstacles and achieve her goals. Through her encounters with the Scarecrow, the Tin Woodman, and the Cowardly Lion, Dorothy discovers that true strength comes from within and that the heart is the most powerful force of all.

"The Heart of Humans" also highlights the importance of friendship and the impact it can have on our lives. As Dorothy forms deep connections with her companions, she realizes the value of genuine relationships and the support they provide. The book reminds us that we are not alone in our journey through life, and that the bonds we form with others can offer comfort, guidance, and a sense of belonging.

Furthermore, "The Heart of Humans" explores the concept of home and the longing we all have for a place where we feel safe, loved, and accepted. Through Dorothy's longing for Kansas, the book reminds us of the significance of finding our place in the world and the importance of cherishing the environments and communities that nurture us.

Overall, "The Heart of Humans" is a timeless and enchanting tale that invites readers to reflect on their own journey of self-discovery and personal growth. It encourages us to embrace the power of belief, kindness, and empathy, and to cultivate meaningful connections with others. Through its captivating narrative and profound themes, the book inspires us to listen to the whispers of our own hearts and to embark on a transformative journey towards authenticity, fulfillment, and true happiness.

Purpose of humans

The purpose of humans is a profound and multifaceted concept that has captivated the minds and hearts of individuals throughout history. It is a question that has been pondered by philosophers, theologians, and thinkers from various cultural, religious, and philosophical backgrounds. While the question of human purpose may not have a definitive, universally accepted answer, it is a topic that invites exploration and contemplation.

From a religious perspective, many belief systems posit that humans have a predetermined purpose or a divine plan that is bestowed upon them by a higher power or deity. Within these frameworks, the purpose of humans may involve serving and worshiping the divine, following moral principles and commandments, or fulfilling a specific role or mission in the world. The purpose of humans, in this context, may be intertwined with concepts of salvation, enlightenment, or spiritual growth. It can be seen as a journey of aligning one's actions, thoughts, and beliefs with the teachings and principles of the religious tradition to which one adheres.

On the other hand, secular perspectives offer a more subjective and individualistic understanding of human purpose. Without relying on religious or supernatural beliefs, these perspectives suggest that humans have the autonomy and freedom to create their own purpose and find meaning in their lives. This can involve pursuing personal fulfillment, cultivating meaningful relationships, engaging in creative expression, making contributions to society, or seeking personal growth and self-actualization. The purpose of humans, in this context, may be deeply intertwined with personal growth, self-realization, and the pursuit of happiness and fulfillment. It is a journey of self-discovery and self-creation, where individuals have the agency to shape their own lives and determine the meaning and purpose that resonates with them.

Moreover, certain philosophical and existential perspectives propose that the purpose of humans lies in the quest for self-actualization and the realization of their full potential. Drawing from the works of thinkers such as Socrates, Aristotle, and Maslow, these perspectives emphasize the importance of introspection, self-reflection, and the development of one's unique talents, passions, and virtues. The purpose of humans, in this context, may involve exploring and understanding one's own values, passions, and talents, and striving for personal development, fulfillment, and the actualization of one's true self. It is a journey of self-discovery and personal growth, where individuals strive to become the best version of themselves and live a life that is aligned with their true nature and potential.

It is important to recognize that the purpose of humans is a deeply personal and individual journey. It is influenced by a multitude of factors, including cultural, religious, and societal beliefs, as well as personal values, experiences, and aspirations. Finding one's purpose often involves introspection, self-reflection, and a search for meaning and fulfillment in life. It may require exploring one's passions, talents, and values, and aligning them with actions and choices that bring a sense of purpose and meaning. It is a dynamic process that unfolds over time, with new insights and revelations emerging as individuals navigate different stages of life and encounter new challenges and opportunities.

Furthermore, the purpose of humans is not a static concept. It can evolve and change throughout one's life as individuals grow, learn, and experience new things. It is a journey of continuous self-discovery and self-creation, where individuals have the opportunity to redefine and reshape their purpose as they gain new insights and perspectives. The search for purpose can be a lifelong journey, with new insights and revelations emerging as individuals navigate different stages of life and encounter new challenges and opportunities.

In addition to the individual quest for purpose, humans also have the capacity to contribute to the greater good and the well-being of others. Acts of kindness, compassion, and service to others can bring a sense of purpose and fulfillment. Engaging in meaningful work, cultivating positive relationships, and making a positive impact on the world can all be expressions of the purpose of humans.

In conclusion, the purpose of humans is a complex and deeply personal concept that invites contemplation, exploration, and self-reflection. It encompasses a wide range of beliefs, perspectives, and interpretations, from religious and spiritual frameworks to secular and philosophical understandings. Ultimately, the purpose of humans may involve serving a divine plan, finding personal fulfillment, pursuing self-actualization, creating meaning, and contributing to the well-being of others. It is a journey of self-discovery and personal growth, where individuals strive to align their actions, thoughts, and beliefs with their true nature and potential to live a life of meaning and purpose.

Changing our thoughts can have a profound impact on our feelings. This highlights the idea that by changing our thoughts and believing in our own abilities, we can harness our inner strength and achieve our goals. It teaches us that true power comes from within ourselves and that we have the capability to transform our feelings by changing our thoughts.

Dr. Wayne Dyer was a renowned self-help author and motivational speaker who emphasized the power of positive thinking and belief in oneself. He believed that our thoughts shape our reality and that by changing our thoughts, we can change our lives. According to Dr. Dyer, true power comes from within ourselves, and we have the ability to tap into our inner strength and achieve our goals. His teachings align with the message in "The Wizard of Oz," which emphasizes the idea that true power resides within oneself and can be accessed by changing our thoughts and beliefs.

"The Wizard of Oz" and the teachings of Dr. Wayne Dyer both emphasize the power of thoughts and beliefs. They highlight that our thoughts shape our reality and that by changing our thoughts, we can change our lives. They suggest that true power comes from within ourselves, and we have the ability to tap into our inner strength and achieve our goals by harnessing the power of our thoughts.

This message can be seen as positive and empowering, as it encourages individuals to take control of their thoughts and beliefs in order to create positive change in their lives. By recognizing that our thoughts have the power to shape our reality, we can cultivate a positive mindset and focus on achieving our goals.

On the other hand, some may argue that this message can be misleading or oversimplified. While thoughts and beliefs are important, they alone may not guarantee success or overcome all obstacles. External factors and circumstances can also play a significant role in shaping outcomes. It is important to acknowledge the complexities of life and to consider a holistic approach that combines positive thinking with practical actions and perseverance.

It is important to highlight the significance of positive qualities such as kindness, empathy, and genuine connections with others. These qualities are portrayed as essential for personal growth and self-discovery. The text suggests that nurturing and protecting the love within oneself and extending it to others is a positive desire, while selfishness and harmful intentions are considered negative desires.

Moreover, it is worth noting the emphasis placed on the power of positive qualities and actions. The text encourages individuals to actively cultivate good desires and strive for personal growth. It also emphasizes the importance of fostering meaningful connections with others, as these connections can greatly contribute to one's overall well-being and fulfillment.

Intuition

Intuition is a remarkable and mysterious aspect of human cognition that goes beyond the realm of conscious reasoning and logical analysis. It is an innate and instinctual ability that allows individuals to understand or know something without relying on external evidence or rational thinking. Often described as a "gut feeling" or a sense of knowing, intuition operates on a deeper level of consciousness, accessing information and insights that may not be readily available to our conscious awareness.

One of the fascinating aspects of intuition is its capacity to guide decision-making. In situations where time is limited or information is incomplete, intuition can serve as a reliable compass, providing us with a sense of what feels right or aligned with our true selves. It taps into our unconscious knowledge and experiences, drawing on a vast reservoir of information that our conscious mind may not be aware of. By trusting our intuition, we can make decisions that are in harmony with our values, aspirations, and intuition can be a valuable guide in navigating through complex and uncertain situations.

Intuition also plays a vital role in problem-solving and creative thinking. It allows us to make connections and see patterns that may not be immediately apparent through logical analysis alone. Intuitive insights often arise from a synthesis of various pieces of information, experiences, and emotions, leading to innovative solutions and fresh perspectives. By tapping into our intuition, we can access our innate creativity and uncover novel approaches to challenges and obstacles.

Furthermore, intuition can be a powerful tool for personal growth and self-discovery. It can guide us in uncovering our true desires, passions, and purpose in life. Intuition helps us bypass societal expectations and external influences, allowing us to connect with our authentic selves and make choices that align with our deepest values and aspirations. By listening to our intuition, we can embark on a profound journey of self-exploration, self-acceptance, and personal transformation.

Cultivating and nurturing our intuition requires practice and self-awareness. It involves developing a heightened sense of mindfulness and attunement to our inner voice and bodily sensations. By creating space for silence, reflection, and introspection in our lives, we can enhance our receptivity to intuitive insights. Practices such as meditation, journaling, and spending time in nature can help us quiet our minds and open ourselves to the wisdom that intuition offers.

It is important to note that while intuition is a valuable resource, it is not infallible. It is essential to balance intuitive insights with critical thinking and rational analysis. Intuition should be used in conjunction with evidence-based decision-making and a comprehensive understanding of the situation at hand. By integrating intuition with logic and reason, we can make well-informed decisions that take into account both our intuitive wisdom and the practical realities of the situation.

In conclusion, intuition is a fascinating and powerful aspect of human cognition. It allows us to tap into our innate wisdom, make confident decisions, and find innovative solutions to problems. By cultivating and trusting our intuition, we can embark on a journey of self-discovery, personal growth, and creative exploration. Intuition is a valuable tool that can guide us towards a more fulfilling and authentic life, enabling us to navigate the complexities of existence with greater clarity, wisdom, and purpose.

Wisdom

Wisdom, often regarded as the highest form of human understanding, is a profound and multifaceted concept that transcends mere knowledge and intelligence. It encompasses a wide range of qualities, virtues, and attributes that enable individuals to navigate life with insight, discernment, and purpose. Wisdom is the culmination of a lifelong journey of learning, self-reflection, and personal growth, and it empowers individuals to make informed decisions, cultivate meaningful relationships, and contribute positively to the world around them.

At its essence, wisdom involves more than simply acquiring information or facts. It is about gaining a deep and profound understanding of oneself, others, and the world. Wisdom requires introspection, self-awareness, and a willingness to explore the depths of one's own thoughts, emotions, and beliefs. It involves recognizing and acknowledging one's own limitations, biases, and blind spots, and actively seeking to expand one's perspective through continuous learning and self-reflection.

Wisdom also encompasses the ability to discern truth from falsehood, to separate what is essential from what is superficial. It involves developing critical thinking skills, evaluating information critically, and questioning assumptions and beliefs. Wise individuals have the capacity to analyze complex situations, consider multiple perspectives, and arrive at well-informed judgments. They are able to see beyond immediate appearances and delve into the underlying causes and effects of events, allowing them to make decisions that are grounded in wisdom and foresight.

Moreover, wisdom is deeply intertwined with emotional intelligence. It involves understanding and managing one's own emotions, as well as empathizing with the emotions of others. Wise individuals possess a high degree of emotional awareness, allowing them to navigate interpersonal relationships with sensitivity, empathy, and compassion. They are skilled at resolving conflicts, fostering understanding, and building bridges between people. Their emotional intelligence enables them to create harmonious connections and foster a sense of unity and collaboration.

Wisdom also entails a deep respect for the interconnectedness of all beings and the natural world. Wise individuals recognize the profound impact of their actions on others and the environment. They prioritize ethical considerations, social responsibility, and sustainability in their decision-making. They strive to contribute positively to the well-being of others and to leave a positive legacy for future generations. Their wisdom guides them to make choices that align with their values and promote the greater good, fostering a more just, compassionate, and harmonious society.

Furthermore, wisdom is not limited to intellectual pursuits or academic achievements. It is a holistic concept that encompasses spiritual, moral, and ethical dimensions. Wise individuals cultivate a sense of purpose, meaning, and values that guide their actions and decisions. They have a deep appreciation for the beauty and interconnectedness of life, and they actively seek to align their lives with their deepest principles and aspirations. Their wisdom is grounded in a sense of integrity, authenticity, and alignment with their true selves.

In summary, wisdom is a profound and multidimensional concept that goes beyond mere knowledge and intelligence. It involves a deep understanding of oneself, others, and the world, and the ability to apply that understanding in a way that promotes personal growth, meaningful relationships, and positive change. Wisdom requires continuous learning, self-reflection, and the cultivation of emotional intelligence. It encompasses ethical considerations, social responsibility, and a deep respect for the interconnectedness of all beings. Ultimately, wisdom empowers individuals to live with purpose, integrity, and compassion, contributing to the betterment of themselves, others, and the world as a whole.

Embracing good

Embracing goodness is a profound and life-altering journey that invites us to explore the depths of our own humanity and tap into the vast reservoir of love, compassion, and kindness that resides within us. When we choose to embrace goodness as a guiding principle in our lives, we embark on a transformative path that not only elevates our own well-being but also has the potential to create a ripple effect of positive change in the world.

At its core, embracing goodness is about cultivating a deep sense of awareness and intentionality in our thoughts, words, and actions. It is about consciously choosing to align ourselves with values such as empathy, integrity, respect, and altruism. By embracing these virtues, we become more attuned to the needs and experiences of others, and we develop a genuine desire to contribute to the well-being and happiness of those around us.

Embracing goodness goes beyond mere acts of kindness or momentary displays of compassion. It is a way of life, a state of being that permeates every aspect of our existence. It is reflected in the way we treat ourselves, how we interact with others, and the choices we make on a daily basis. It is about fostering a mindset of gratitude, forgiveness, and non-judgment, and extending these qualities not only to ourselves but to others.

When we embrace goodness, we create a positive and nurturing environment that fosters growth, connection, and understanding. Our actions and attitudes become a source of inspiration for those around us, encouraging them to embrace their own goodness and to make choices that align with their highest values. By embodying goodness, we become catalysts for positive change in the world, igniting a collective movement towards a more compassionate, just, and harmonious society.

Embracing goodness also involves recognizing and addressing the challenges and obstacles that may hinder our ability to fully embody these virtues. It requires us to confront and transform our own biases, prejudices, and conditioned patterns of thinking and behaving. It calls us to cultivate self-awareness and to engage in continuous self-reflection and personal growth. Through this process, we can uncover and release the layers of negativity, fear, and self-centeredness that may prevent us from fully embracing and expressing our inherent goodness.

Embracing goodness is not a solitary endeavor. It thrives in the context of community and collaboration. When we come together with others who share a similar commitment to goodness, we amplify our impact and create a collective force for positive change. Through meaningful connections, open dialogue, and collaborative action, we can co-create a world that reflects and embodies the highest aspirations of humanity.

In conclusion, embracing goodness is a profound and transformative journey that invites us to tap into the boundless reservoir of love, compassion, and kindness within ourselves. It is a way of life that calls us to align our thoughts, words, and actions with virtues such as empathy, integrity, respect, and altruism. By embracing goodness, we become catalysts for positive change in the world, creating a ripple effect of love, compassion, and understanding. Let us embark on this journey of embracing goodness and work together to create a world that reflects the inherent goodness of humanity.

The inherent goodness of humans is a deeply ingrained and multifaceted aspect of our existence that extends beyond individual actions and behaviors. It encompasses our ability to connect with one another on a profound level, to empathize with the experiences of others, and to strive for the greater good of humanity as a whole.

At the very essence of our being, humans possess an innate capacity for love, compassion, and kindness. This inherent goodness is rooted in our shared humanity and our interconnectedness with all living beings. It is a reflection of our inherent dignity and worth as individuals, and it forms the basis for our moral and ethical principles.

The belief in the inherent goodness of humans is supported by various philosophical, religious, and spiritual traditions. Many belief systems affirm that humans are created in the image of a divine source, imbued with a spark of divinity that manifests as our capacity for goodness. This belief serves as a guiding principle for cultivating virtues such as empathy, generosity, and forgiveness, and encourages us to strive for personal growth and ethical conduct.

Furthermore, scientific research in fields such as psychology, neuroscience, and social sciences has provided empirical evidence for the existence of human goodness. Studies have shown that acts of kindness and compassion not only benefit the recipients but also have a positive impact on the well-being and happiness of the individuals who perform them. This suggests that our inherent goodness is not only beneficial for others but also contributes to our own personal fulfillment and flourishing.

The belief in human goodness is also reflected in the countless examples of individuals who have dedicated their lives to serving others and making a positive impact on the world. From influential leaders and activists to everyday heroes, these individuals have demonstrated the immense capacity of humans to overcome adversity, show resilience in the face of challenges, and inspire positive change. Their actions serve as a testament to the transformative power of human goodness and the potential for greatness that resides within each and every one of us.

It is important to acknowledge that humans are not immune to negative behaviors and actions. We are susceptible to the influence of external factors such as societal pressures, cultural norms, and personal circumstances that can sometimes lead us astray from our inherent goodness. However, even in the face of these challenges, humans have the ability to reflect, learn, and grow. We can choose to cultivate virtues such as empathy, compassion, and integrity, and strive to align our actions with our inherent goodness.

The belief in human goodness has profound implications for how we view ourselves, others, and the world around us. When we recognize and embrace the inherent goodness in ourselves and others, we foster an environment of trust, respect, and understanding. It encourages us to approach conflicts with empathy and compassion, seeking peaceful resolutions and reconciliation. By nurturing the belief in human goodness, we can build harmonious relationships, strong communities, and a more just and compassionate society.

In conclusion, the belief in the inherent goodness of humans is a powerful and transformative perspective that recognizes our capacity for love, compassion, and kindness. It is supported by philosophical, religious, and scientific evidence, and is reflected in the actions of individuals who have dedicated their lives to serving others. While negative behaviors may exist, our inherent goodness remains a fundamental aspect of our nature. Let us embrace and nurture this goodness within ourselves and others, and work together to create a world where love, compassion, and kindness prevail.

Harmony

The concept of "harmony" can be seen throughout "The Wizard of Oz." As Dorothy embarks on her journey to find her way back home, she encounters various characters who join her in her quest. Despite their differences, Dorothy and her companions, the Scarecrow, the Tin Woodman, and the Cowardly Lion, learn to work together and support one another. Through their collaboration and unity, they are able to overcome challenges and achieve their goals. This theme of harmony highlights the importance of cooperation, understanding, and finding common ground in order to create a harmonious and successful outcome.

The concept of Jesus and profits being in harmony is a profound and thought-provoking topic that invites us to delve deeper into the intersection of spirituality, economics, and ethics. It requires us to explore the teachings of Jesus, the values and principles of Christianity, and the ethical considerations surrounding the pursuit of wealth in today's society.

In Christianity, Jesus is often portrayed as a compassionate and selfless figure who emphasized the importance of spiritual values and the well-being of others. His teachings focused on love, compassion, and service to others. Jesus challenged societal norms and called for a radical transformation of hearts and minds. He spoke against the love of money, greed, and the exploitation of others for personal gain.

However, this does not mean that Jesus condemned the pursuit of profits or financial success in and of itself. Rather, Jesus emphasized the intention and values behind the pursuit of wealth. He taught that material possessions should not be the ultimate goal in life, but rather a means to serve others and contribute to the greater good. Jesus encouraged his followers to use their resources responsibly and generously, to care for the poor and marginalized, and to seek justice and righteousness in all aspects of life.

In Christian teachings, it is believed that individuals should use their resources, including financial resources, responsibly and in ways that align with their faith. This includes being good stewards of wealth, practicing generosity, and using profits for the betterment of society. Many Christians view business and entrepreneurship as opportunities to create value, provide employment, and positively impact their communities.

The harmonization of Jesus and profits requires a holistic approach that integrates spiritual values, ethical considerations, and an understanding of the complexities of the modern economic system. It involves aligning one's financial endeavors with the teachings of Jesus, practicing ethical business principles, and using profits to promote justice, equality, and the well-being of all people.

At the same time, it is crucial to acknowledge that the pursuit of profits can be accompanied by ethical challenges and temptations. The desire for wealth and success can lead to greed, exploitation, and the neglect of moral responsibilities. Christians are called to be discerning and vigilant, to examine their motives and actions, and to ensure that their pursuit of profits does not compromise their commitment to love, justice, and compassion.

The relationship between Jesus and profits also necessitates a critical examination of the economic systems and structures that perpetuate inequality and injustice. Christians are called to challenge unjust economic practices, advocate for fair wages and working conditions, and work towards a more equitable distribution of resources. This may involve supporting initiatives that promote economic empowerment, sustainable development, and social entrepreneurship.

Furthermore, the harmonization of Jesus and profits extends beyond individual actions to the collective responsibility of society. It requires a reevaluation of societal priorities and values, a commitment to addressing systemic injustices, and a willingness to challenge the status quo. Christians are called to advocate for economic systems that prioritize human dignity, social justice, and the flourishing of all people.

Ultimately, the harmonization of Jesus and profits is an ongoing journey of personal and collective transformation. It requires individuals to continually reflect upon their actions, examine their intentions, and seek guidance from the teachings of Jesus and the wisdom of their faith tradition. It is through this process of self-reflection, prayer, and ethical discernment that individuals can strive to find harmony between their financial pursuits and their commitment to live out the values of love, justice, and compassion taught by Jesus.

It is important to note that interpretations of the relationship between Jesus and profits may vary among different Christian denominations and individuals. The teachings of Jesus and their application to the pursuit of profits are subjects of ongoing theological, ethical, and economic discussions within Christian communities. It is through respectful dialogue, open-mindedness, and a commitment to the common good that individuals can engage in meaningful conversations and work towards a more harmonious integration of Jesus and profits in our lives and society.

Harmony is an essential and fundamental aspect of human existence that encompasses various dimensions of our lives. It is not only important on an individual level but also has profound implications for interpersonal relationships, communities, and the world at large.

At an individual level, harmony plays a significant role in promoting inner peace, balance, and well-being. When we achieve harmony within ourselves, we experience a sense of alignment between our thoughts, emotions, and actions. This state of inner harmony allows us to live authentically, make choices that align with our values and aspirations, and cultivate a deep sense of self-acceptance and contentment.

In interpersonal relationships, harmony is vital for fostering healthy connections and meaningful interactions. When there is harmony between individuals, there is a sense of mutual respect, understanding, and empathy. It enables effective communication, conflict resolution, and cooperation. Harmonious relationships are characterized by trust, support, and the ability to navigate challenges together. They provide a source of emotional support, companionship, and a sense of belonging.

On a broader scale, harmony within communities and societies is crucial for creating a peaceful, inclusive, and thriving environment. When there is harmony within a community, there is a collective sense of unity, cooperation, and shared values. It encourages social cohesion, collaboration, and a willingness to work towards the common good. Harmonious communities are characterized by respect for diversity, social justice, and the promotion of equality and human rights.

Harmony also extends to our relationship with the natural world. It involves recognizing and respecting the interconnectedness and interdependence of all living beings and the environment. When there is harmony between humanity and nature, there is a deep sense of reverence, stewardship, and sustainable practices. It involves living in harmony with nature, taking actions to preserve and protect the planet, and ensuring the well-being of future generations.

Moreover, harmony is important in promoting global peace, understanding, and cooperation. In a world that is increasingly interconnected and interdependent, achieving global harmony is essential for addressing global challenges such as poverty, inequality, and climate change. It requires fostering dialogue, promoting cultural exchange, and embracing the principles of diplomacy and conflict resolution. Global harmony involves recognizing our shared humanity, respecting diverse perspectives, and working towards a more just, peaceful, and sustainable world.

In summary, harmony is a multifaceted concept that holds immense importance in various aspects of our lives. It contributes to our individual well-being, fosters healthy relationships, creates harmonious communities, promotes environmental sustainability, and plays a crucial role in achieving global peace and cooperation. By cultivating harmony within ourselves and in our interactions with others and the world, we can contribute to a more harmonious and thriving existence for all.

Emotions

Emotion is a multifaceted and intricate phenomenon that encompasses a wide range of psychological and physiological processes. It plays a fundamental role in shaping our experiences, behaviors, and overall well-being.

At its core, emotion refers to a complex interplay of subjective feelings, thoughts, and bodily responses. It represents our internal reactions to various stimuli, situations, or events, and influences how we perceive and interact with the world around us.

Emotions are often categorized into basic or primary emotions, such as joy, anger, fear, sadness, surprise, and disgust. These basic emotions are considered to be universally experienced across cultures and are thought to have evolved as adaptive responses to specific situations. For example, fear helps us respond to potential threats, while joy enhances our motivation and reward-seeking behaviors.

However, emotions are not limited to these basic categories. They exist on a spectrum and can manifest in various combinations and intensities. Complex emotions, such as love, jealousy, guilt, shame, pride, and awe, arise from the interplay of multiple basic emotions and cognitive processes.

Emotions involve a complex interplay of various components:

1. Subjective Experience: Emotions are accompanied by subjective feelings and sensations that range from subtle to intense. These feelings provide us with a unique and personal experience of the emotion. For example, joy may be experienced as a sense of happiness and excitement, while sadness may be experienced as a deep feeling of sorrow or grief.

2. Physiological Response: Emotions are associated with physiological changes in the body. These changes include alterations in heart rate, blood pressure, breathing patterns, hormonal activity, and activation of the autonomic nervous system. For instance, fear may lead to increased heart rate, sweaty palms, and heightened alertness in preparation for a potential threat.

3. Cognitive Appraisal: Emotions involve cognitive processes that help us evaluate and interpret situations. Our thoughts, beliefs, and interpretations of events influence the emotions we experience. For example, if we perceive a situation as threatening, we may feel fear or anxiety. Cognitive appraisal also plays a role in determining the intensity and duration of emotional responses.

4. Expressive Behavior: Emotions can be expressed through facial expressions, body language, vocal tone, and verbal communication. These expressions serve as nonverbal cues that convey our internal emotional states to others. For instance, a smile can indicate happiness or amusement, while a frown can signal sadness or displeasure.

Emotions serve several important functions in our lives:

1. Adaptive Response: Emotions help us respond and adapt to our environment. They provide valuable information about potential threats or opportunities. For example, fear can alert

us to danger and prompt us to take protective actions, while joy can reinforce behaviors that lead to positive outcomes.

2. Social Interaction: Emotions play a crucial role in social communication and interaction. They provide important signals to others about our feelings, intentions, and needs. Emotions help us understand and respond to the emotions of others, fostering empathy, connection, and cooperation.

3. Decision-Making: Emotions influence our decision-making processes by providing us with information about our preferences, values, and desires. They can guide our choices and actions by signaling what is important or rewarding to us. For example, excitement and anticipation may motivate us to pursue a particular goal or take risks.

4. Well-being: Emotions contribute to our overall psychological well-being and can influence our subjective happiness and life satisfaction. Positive emotions, such as joy, gratitude, and contentment, are associated with greater well-being, while excessive or prolonged negative emotions can have detrimental effects on our mental and physical health.

Understanding and managing emotions is a crucial aspect of emotional intelligence. It involves recognizing, interpreting, and regulating our own emotions, as well as understanding and empathizing with the emotions of others. Developing emotional intelligence can contribute to personal growth, self-awareness, effective communication, and the building of meaningful relationships.

It is important to note that emotions are complex and can vary greatly between individuals and cultures. They can also be influenced by various factors, such as personal experiences, cultural norms, and individual differences. Additionally, emotions are not inherently good or bad but are informative signals that provide valuable information about our inner and outer experiences.

By cultivating emotional intelligence and developing a deeper understanding of our emotions, we can navigate our lives with greater self-awareness, empathy, and resilience. Emotions are an integral part of the human experience and embracing them allows us to lead more fulfilling and authentic lives.

Prayer

Prayer is a timeless and universal practice that holds profound significance in the lives of humans across cultures, religions, and spiritual traditions. It is a deeply personal and sacred act of communication with the divine or a higher power, serving as a means to connect with the transcendent, seek guidance and solace, express gratitude, and cultivate a profound sense of inner peace and spiritual fulfillment.

Throughout history, prayer has been an integral part of human existence, providing a pathway for individuals to transcend the limitations of the physical world and tap into the infinite realm of the divine. It is a practice that allows humans to express their deepest thoughts, emotions, desires, and fears, knowing that they are heard and understood by a benevolent and compassionate presence.

At its core, prayer reflects the innate human longing for connection, purpose, and meaning. It is a way for individuals to establish a personal relationship with the divine, regardless of their religious or spiritual beliefs. Through prayer, humans can experience a deep sense of belonging, find solace in times of struggle, and gain clarity and guidance in navigating the complexities of life.

Prayer takes on many forms, ranging from recitation of sacred texts, chanting, meditation, visualization, contemplation, or simply speaking the words of the heart. It can be practiced individually in private spaces, within the confines of a religious institution, or in communal gatherings. Regardless of the method or setting, prayer serves as a powerful conduit for communion with the divine, allowing humans to transcend the confines of the material world and access the realm of the sacred.

One of the fundamental purposes of prayer is to seek guidance and wisdom from the divine. Through prayer, individuals can find clarity amidst confusion, answers to their questions, and direction in their lives. It is a means to align one's thoughts, intentions, and actions with a higher purpose, seeking divine insight and inspiration to make choices that are in harmony with one's values and aspirations.

Prayer also plays a crucial role in cultivating a sense of gratitude and appreciation. It provides a space for individuals to express their thankfulness for the blessings in their lives, recognizing the abundance and beauty that surrounds them. Gratitude prayers can foster a positive mindset, promote feelings of contentment and joy, and cultivate a deep sense of interconnectedness and humility.

Moreover, prayer serves as a refuge of solace, strength, and healing during times of difficulty, pain, or loss. It offers a sanctuary for individuals to express their deepest emotions, find comfort in the midst of challenges, and experience a profound sense of hope and resilience. Prayer can provide solace, peace, and a sense of surrender, helping individuals find inner strength and courage to navigate life's hardships.

Beyond its personal benefits, prayer has the power to foster unity, compassion, and social transformation. Communal prayers and interfaith gatherings bring people together, transcending differences and fostering a sense of shared purpose and interconnectedness. Prayer can inspire individuals to act with compassion, empathy, and justice, motivating them to address societal issues, work towards peace, and alleviate suffering in the world.

Furthermore, prayer serves as a catalyst for personal and spiritual growth. It is a doorway to self-reflection, introspection, and a deepening of one's relationship with the divine. Through prayer, humans can cultivate qualities such as humility, patience, forgiveness, and love, fostering a profound transformation within themselves and radiating that transformation outward to others.

It is important to recognize that prayer is not confined to specific religious or spiritual traditions. It is a universal human experience that transcends cultural boundaries and can be practiced by individuals from all walks of life. Prayer has the potential to bridge divides, promote understanding, and encourage dialogue and cooperation among diverse communities.

In conclusion, prayer is a timeless and sacred practice that allows humans to connect with the divine, seek guidance, express gratitude, find solace, and contribute to personal and collective transformation. It is an integral part of the human experience, reflecting our innate spiritual nature and longing for transcendence. Through prayer, individuals can cultivate a deeper sense of self-awareness, find comfort and strength in challenging times, and foster unity, compassion, and love in their interactions with others and the world around them.

Thankfulness

Thankfulness is a profound and transformative practice that invites us to cultivate a mindset of gratitude and appreciation for the blessings and positive aspects of our lives. It is a practice that goes beyond mere politeness or social courtesy, and instead encourages us to actively recognize, acknowledge, and express gratitude for the abundance and beauty that surrounds us.

When we practice thankfulness, we develop a heightened sense of awareness and mindfulness, allowing us to shift our focus towards the positive aspects of our lives. It is about finding joy in the simplest of things, whether it's a beautiful sunset, a kind gesture from a stranger, or a moment of peace and tranquility. By cultivating thankfulness, we train our minds to seek out the positive and to recognize the blessings that are often overlooked or taken for granted.

The practice of thankfulness has been shown to have numerous benefits for our overall well-being. Research has found that individuals who regularly engage in gratitude exercises experience lower levels of stress, anxiety, and depression. They also report higher levels of life satisfaction, optimism, and resilience. Cultivating a mindset of thankfulness can have a profound impact on our mental and emotional health, allowing us to navigate life's challenges with greater ease and positivity.

In addition to its positive effects on our well-being, thankfulness also plays a significant role in our relationships with others. When we express gratitude towards the people in our lives, whether it's a friend, family member, colleague, or even a stranger, we not only make them feel valued and appreciated, but we also strengthen the bonds of connection and foster a sense of belonging. Thankfulness has the power to deepen our relationships, promote empathy and understanding, and create a supportive and harmonious social environment.

Furthermore, the practice of thankfulness can extend beyond our immediate relationships and have a broader impact on our communities and society. When we express gratitude for the efforts and contributions of others, whether it's a teacher, healthcare worker, volunteer, or any individual working towards the betterment of society, we uplift and inspire those around us. Thankfulness has the power to create a ripple effect of positivity, kindness, and compassion, fostering a culture of appreciation, support, and collaboration.

Practicing thankfulness can take many forms, and there are various techniques and exercises that can help us cultivate a mindset of gratitude. Keeping a gratitude journal, where we write down the things, we are thankful for each day, can be a powerful practice that allows us to reflect on the positive aspects of our lives. Taking a moment each day to pause, breathe, and express gratitude for the present moment can also be a simple yet profound practice. Additionally, expressing gratitude through words, acts of kindness, or even small gestures can have a significant impact on both ourselves and those around us.

Moreover, thankfulness has the power to transform our perspective and outlook on life. When we approach each day with a grateful heart, we open ourselves up to the wonders and possibilities that exist in every moment. We become more attuned to the beauty and goodness in the world, and we develop a greater sense of contentment and fulfillment. Thankfulness allows us to embrace the present moment and find joy in the simple pleasures of life, leading to a more meaningful and fulfilling existence.

In conclusion, thankfulness is a transformative practice that invites us to cultivate a mindset of gratitude and appreciation. It has numerous benefits for our mental and emotional well-being, strengthens our relationships, and contributes to a more positive and compassionate society. By actively practicing thankfulness, we can shift our focus towards the positive aspects of our lives, foster a sense of contentment and fulfillment, and contribute to a more harmonious and grateful world.

Human Proverbs

Human proverbs, often referred to as "words of wisdom," are a treasure trove of knowledge that has been passed down through generations. These age-old sayings encapsulate the collective experiences, observations, and values of humanity, offering guidance and insight into various aspects of life.

Proverbs serve as concise and memorable expressions of wisdom, capturing profound truths about human nature, relationships, personal growth, and societal values. They are like distilled drops of wisdom that have stood the test of time, resonating with people across cultures and generations.

One such proverb is "Actions speak louder than words." This proverb reminds us that our actions carry more weight and reveal our true character more effectively than mere words. It emphasizes the importance of aligning our actions with our intentions, highlighting the significance of integrity, consistency, and authenticity. By focusing on our actions, we demonstrate our commitment and build trust with others.

Another well-known human proverb is "A stitch in time saves nine." This proverb underscores the value of timely action and proactive problem-solving. It encourages us to address challenges and issues promptly, as early intervention can prevent them from escalating into larger and more complicated problems. By taking timely action, we save ourselves from unnecessary stress, difficulties, and potentially greater consequences.

The proverb "Honesty is the best policy" speaks to the fundamental importance of truthfulness and integrity in our interactions and relationships. It reminds us that honesty forms the foundation of trust, fostering open communication, and deepening connections with others. Upholding honesty cultivates personal integrity, strengthens relationships, and contributes to a harmonious society.

Human proverbs encompass a wide range of topics and themes, including love, perseverance, resilience, and gratitude. For example, "Love conquers all" emphasizes the transformative power of love in overcoming challenges and uniting people. "Fall seven times, stand up eight" encourages resilience and the willingness to persevere in the face of adversity. "Gratitude turns what we have into enough" reminds us to appreciate and find contentment in the present moment.

Beyond offering practical guidance, human proverbs reflect the cultural values and beliefs of the societies from which they originate. They provide insights into the shared wisdom and experiences of a community, and they contribute to the preservation of cultural identity and heritage.

Human proverbs serve as moral compasses, guiding us in making ethical decisions and shaping our character. They encapsulate universal truths and enduring principles that have stood the test of time. By reflecting on and applying these proverbs, we can gain wisdom, navigate challenges, and lead more meaningful and fulfilling lives.

In conclusion, human proverbs are invaluable gems of wisdom that offer timeless guidance and insight into various aspects of life. They reflect the collective experiences, values, and observations of humanity, providing us with practical wisdom and moral compasses to navigate the complexities of life. By embracing and applying these proverbs, we can cultivate virtue, make wiser choices, and contribute to a more harmonious and compassionate world.

Humanities

"There is no life without humanities" conveys the profound and indispensable role that humanities play in every aspect of our existence. Humanities encompass a vast array of disciplines, including literature, history, philosophy, art, music, language, cultural studies, and more. These disciplines provide us with the tools to explore, interpret, and appreciate the complexities of the human experience, enabling us to understand our past, navigate our present, and shape our future.

Literature, for example, allows us to immerse ourselves in the stories, ideas, and emotions of characters from different time periods and cultures. Through the power of storytelling, we gain insights into the human condition, exploring themes of love, loss, resilience, and the pursuit of meaning. Literature fosters empathy, as it enables us to step into the shoes of others and understand their perspectives, broadening our horizons and deepening our understanding of humanity.

History, on the other hand, provides us with a lens through which we can examine the events, people, and societal forces that have shaped our world. By studying history, we gain a sense of continuity and connection with those who came before us. We learn from past successes and failures, allowing us to make informed decisions and contribute to the progress of society. History provides us with a collective memory, preserving the stories and lessons of our ancestors and shaping our identity as individuals and communities.

Philosophy delves into the fundamental questions of existence, ethics, knowledge, and reality. It encourages us to critically examine our beliefs, values, and assumptions, fostering intellectual curiosity and a deeper understanding of ourselves and the world around us. Philosophy challenges us to think deeply, grapple with complex ideas, and develop our own reasoned perspectives. It equips us with the tools to navigate moral dilemmas, ethical challenges, and existential questions.

Art, in its myriad forms, serves as a powerful expression of the human spirit and imagination. Through painting, sculpture, music, dance, theater, and film, artists capture the essence of human emotions, experiences, and aspirations. Art stimulates our senses, evokes deep emotions, and provokes meaningful contemplation. It has the power to transcend linguistic and cultural barriers, speaking to our shared humanity and connecting us on a profound level.

The humanities also cultivate essential skills and competencies that are valuable in all aspects of life. They foster critical thinking, analytical reasoning, and problem-solving abilities. Humanities disciplines emphasize the importance of evidence-based arguments, logical reasoning, and the ability to evaluate information critically. They teach us to question assumptions, challenge established norms, and explore alternative perspectives.

Moreover, the humanities contribute to the development of effective communication skills. Through the study of literature, philosophy, and art, we learn to articulate our thoughts and emotions, express ourselves eloquently, and engage in meaningful dialogue. The humanities cultivate empathy and open-mindedness, enabling us to understand and appreciate diverse perspectives and promote inclusivity and social justice.

Beyond their individual benefits, the humanities have a profound impact on society as a whole. They foster cultural appreciation, promote cross-cultural understanding, and bridge divides between different communities. The humanities encourage us to recognize and celebrate the richness and diversity of human cultures, fostering mutual respect and global citizenship. They contribute to the formation of informed and engaged citizens who are equipped to address complex societal challenges and promote positive change.

In conclusion, the statement "There is no life without humanities" encapsulates the vital role that humanities play in our lives. They broaden our horizons, deepen our understanding of ourselves and others, and equip us with the skills and knowledge necessary to navigate the complexities of our world. The humanities nurture empathy, critical thinking, and effective communication, fostering personal growth, societal progress, and the pursuit of a more enlightened and inclusive future.

Memories

Memory is the ability of the brain to store, retain, and recall information and experiences. It plays a crucial role in our daily lives, allowing us to learn, make decisions, and navigate the world around us. The brain's memory system is complex and involves multiple processes and structures.

There are different types of memory, including short-term memory, long-term memory, and working memory. Short-term memory refers to the temporary storage of information that lasts for seconds to minutes. It allows us to hold and manipulate information in our minds for immediate use. Long-term memory involves the storage of information for longer periods, potentially for a lifetime. It is responsible for retaining knowledge, experiences, and skills acquired over time. Working memory is a system that allows us to hold and manipulate information in our minds while performing cognitive tasks.

Memory formation involves three main stages: encoding, consolidation, and retrieval. During encoding, information is received and transformed into a form that can be stored in the brain. Consolidation is the process of stabilizing and strengthening the memory traces in the brain, making them more resistant to forgetting. Retrieval is the process of accessing and recalling stored information when needed.

The brain's memory system relies on the coordinated activity of different brain regions, including the hippocampus, amygdala, and prefrontal cortex. The hippocampus plays a crucial role in the formation and retrieval of declarative memories, which are memories of facts and events. The amygdala is involved in the processing and storage of emotional memories. The prefrontal cortex is responsible for working memory and the organization and manipulation of information.

The brain's memory capacity is vast and can store a vast amount of information. However, not all memories are equally accessible or well-preserved. Factors such as attention, rehearsal, emotional significance, and repetition can influence the formation and retention of memories. Forgetting can occur due to decay, interference, or retrieval failure.

Overall, the brain's memory system is a fundamental aspect of human cognition that allows us to acquire, retain, and retrieve information. It is a dynamic and complex process that continues to be a topic of study and exploration in neuroscience and psychology.

True power comes by changing our thoughts and beliefs, we can overcome challenges and achieve our goals.

True power comes from within ourselves. It is the ability to harness our thoughts and beliefs that allows us to overcome challenges and achieve our goals. Our mindset plays a crucial role in shaping our reality and determining the outcomes we experience in life.

When we believe in ourselves and our capabilities, we tap into an inner strength and resilience that propels us forward. By changing our thoughts and beliefs, we can break free from self-imposed limitations and unlock our full potential. We can replace self-doubt with self-confidence, fear with courage, and negative self-talk with positive affirmations.

Changing our thoughts and beliefs requires conscious effort and a willingness to challenge our existing mindset. It involves identifying and questioning limiting beliefs that hold us back and replacing them with empowering and supportive beliefs. For example, instead of believing that we are not capable of achieving our goals, we can adopt the belief that with determination and hard work, anything is possible.

As we shift our thoughts and beliefs, we begin to see opportunities where we once saw obstacles. We become more open to new possibilities and approaches. Challenges that once seemed insurmountable become steppingstones on our path to success. We develop a growth mindset, embracing the idea that failure is not a setback but rather an opportunity for learning and growth.

Moreover, changing our thoughts and beliefs can have a profound impact on our emotions and overall well-being. When we cultivate positive and empowering thoughts, we experience greater happiness, resilience, and inner peace. We become more optimistic and hopeful, even in the face of adversity. Our thoughts shape our emotions, and by changing our thoughts, we can create a more positive and fulfilling emotional landscape.

It is important to note that changing our thoughts and beliefs is not a one-time event but an ongoing process. It requires consistent effort and self-reflection. We must continuously challenge and reevaluate our beliefs, ensuring that they align with our values and aspirations. Surrounding ourselves with positive influences, such as supportive friends, mentors, or role models, can also play a significant role in reinforcing our new mindset.

In addition to personal growth and achievement, changing our thoughts and beliefs can have a ripple effect on those around us. When we embody a positive and empowered mindset, we become a source of inspiration and encouragement for others. Our transformation serves as a beacon of hope and possibility, motivating those around us to also embrace their inner power and pursue their dreams.

Furthermore, changing our thoughts and beliefs can lead to a greater sense of purpose and fulfillment. As we align our thoughts with our values and aspirations, we gain clarity on our life's purpose and the impact we want to make in the world. We become more intentional in our actions, making choices that are in alignment with our authentic selves. This sense of purpose and alignment brings a deep sense of fulfillment and satisfaction.

In conclusion, true power comes from within ourselves. By changing our thoughts and beliefs, we can tap into our inner strength and overcome challenges that stand in the way of our goals. It is through this transformation of mindset that we unlock our full potential and create the life we desire. As we embrace empowering thoughts and beliefs, we open ourselves up to new possibilities, experience greater happiness and resilience, and ultimately achieve success in all areas of our lives. Our transformation not only impacts our own lives, but also inspires and uplifts those around us, creating a ripple effect of positive change in the world.

Know your heart!

Knowing your heart is an essential and lifelong journey of self-discovery and self-understanding. It is a process that involves exploring the depths of your innermost being, unraveling the intricacies of your thoughts, emotions, desires, and values.

When you embark on the path of knowing your heart, you embark on a transformative adventure of self-exploration. You begin to peel back the layers of conditioning, societal expectations, and external influences that have shaped your sense of self. You delve into the core of your being, seeking to understand your true essence and uncover the unique qualities that make you who you are.

This journey of self-discovery often involves introspection and self-reflection. It requires setting aside time for solitude and quiet contemplation, allowing yourself to tune in to the whispers of your heart. Through practices such as meditation, journaling, or engaging in meaningful conversations with trusted confidants, you create space for deep introspection and gain insights into your inner world.

As you deepen your self-awareness, you become attuned to your emotions, both the subtle nuances and the powerful currents that flow within you. You learn to listen to the wisdom of your emotions, understanding that they are messengers guiding you towards alignment with your true self. By embracing and honoring your emotions, you cultivate emotional intelligence and develop a greater capacity for empathy and compassion towards yourself and others.

Knowing your heart also involves exploring your desires and passions. It is about recognizing the activities, pursuits, and relationships that bring you a sense of joy, fulfillment, and purpose. By understanding what truly ignites your soul, you can make choices and create a life that is aligned with your deepest longings. This alignment allows you to tap into your innate strengths and talents, unlocking your full potential and leading to a more meaningful and fulfilling existence.

In addition to exploring your desires, knowing your heart requires an examination of your values and beliefs. It involves questioning the assumptions and conditioning that have shaped your worldview and understanding of the world. By critically evaluating your values and beliefs, you can discern which ones resonate with your authentic self and which ones may need to be reevaluated or released. This process of alignment with your true values empowers you to live a life that is congruent with your deepest convictions and principles.

As you journey towards knowing your heart, you develop a profound sense of self-acceptance and self-love. You recognize that you are a unique and ever-evolving individual, deserving of compassion, kindness, and unconditional acceptance. This self-acceptance fosters a deep sense of inner peace and contentment, allowing you to navigate life's challenges with grace and resilience.

Knowing your heart is not a destination but an ongoing exploration. It requires a commitment to lifelong learning, growth, and self-discovery. The more you know your heart, the more you discover about yourself, and the more you understand the interconnectedness between your inner world and the outer world.

In conclusion, knowing your heart is a transformative and lifelong journey that involves self-reflection, emotional intelligence, and alignment with your true desires and values. It is a process of self-discovery and self-acceptance that leads to greater authenticity, fulfillment, and purpose in life. By knowing your heart, you cultivate a deep connection with yourself and the world around you, allowing you to create a life that is in resonance with your true essence.

The Lion

In "The Wizard of Oz," the character of the Cowardly Lion serves as a powerful symbol of the transformative power of courage. Throughout the story, the Cowardly Lion's journey of self-discovery and personal growth captivates readers and viewers alike, leaving a lasting impression on their hearts and minds.

At the beginning of the story, the Cowardly Lion is introduced as a timid and fearful creature. He yearns for courage, believing that it will provide him with the strength and confidence he desires. However, he soon discovers that courage is not something that can be granted to him by external forces, but rather something that must be found within himself.

As the Cowardly Lion joins Dorothy and her companions on their quest to seek help from the Wizard of Oz, he embarks on a profound inner journey. Along the way, he encounters various obstacles and challenges that test his resolve and push him to confront his fears head-on.

One of the pivotal moments in the Cowardly Lion's journey is when he faces the intimidating and all-powerful Wizard of Oz. Despite his initial hesitation, the Cowardly Lion finds the courage to speak up and express his deepest desires. This moment of vulnerability and honesty not only demonstrates his growth but also serves as a catalyst for the transformation that follows.

Throughout the story, the Cowardly Lion learns valuable lessons about the true nature of courage. He discovers that courage does not mean the absence of fear, but rather the ability to act in spite of it. It is through his willingness to confront his fears and take bold actions that he begins to embody the qualities of a true hero.

As the Cowardly Lion's journey progresses, he is inspired by the bravery and determination of his fellow companions, Dorothy, the Scarecrow, and the Tin Man. Their unwavering support and encouragement help him realize that he is not alone in his quest for courage. Together, they form a strong bond built on trust, friendship, and mutual growth.

As the story reaches its climax, the Cowardly Lion undergoes a profound transformation. Through his experiences and interactions, he learns that true courage comes from within and can be found by embracing vulnerability and facing one's fears. The Cowardly Lion's transformation serves as a powerful reminder that we all have the capacity to find strength and courage within ourselves, regardless of our initial doubts and insecurities.

"The Wizard of Oz" leaves us with a valuable lesson: the journey to courage is not an easy one, but it is a journey worth taking. It invites us to reflect on our own fears and limitations and encourages us to take steps towards personal growth and self-discovery. The Cowardly Lion's story reminds us that true courage is not about being fearless, but about recognizing our fears and finding the strength to overcome them.

In conclusion, the character of the Cowardly Lion in "The Wizard of Oz" exemplifies the transformative power of courage. Through his journey of self-discovery, he learns that courage is not something to be bestowed upon us, but a quality that resides within. The Cowardly Lion's story inspires us to confront our fears, embrace vulnerability, and embark on our own journeys of personal growth and self-discovery.

The Tin Man

"The Tin Woodman" is a beloved character in "The Wizard of Oz" who captivates readers and viewers with his endearing personality and inspiring journey. As a man made entirely of tin, he symbolizes the quest for love and compassion, teaching us valuable lessons about the human condition and the power of the heart.

The Tin Woodman's origin story is both tragic and poignant. Once a human woodcutter, he found himself in unfortunate circumstances that led to the gradual replacement of his body parts with tin ones. Despite his new metallic form, the Tin Woodman retained his capacity for kindness, empathy, and a longing to have a heart. This desire for a heart represents the universal human longing for emotional connection and the profound impact it has on our lives.

Throughout the story, the Tin Woodman's interactions with Dorothy and the other characters reveal the depth of his compassion and selflessness. Despite his perceived lack of a heart, he consistently demonstrates acts of kindness, putting the needs of others before his own. His character serves as a reminder that true strength and goodness come from within, and that empathy and love have the power to transform lives.

As the journey progresses, the Tin Woodman's quest for a heart becomes a central theme. It is through his interactions with Dorothy, the Scarecrow, and the Cowardly Lion that he learns about the nature of love and the importance of emotional connection. Together, they navigate the challenges of the Land of Oz, relying on each other's unique strengths and forming unbreakable bonds of friendship. Through their shared experiences, they discover that love and compassion are not limited to physical attributes, but are qualities that reside within the heart.

The symbolic moment of the Tin Woodman receiving a heart made of silk from the Wizard of Oz is a powerful representation of his transformation. It signifies that love and compassion are not gifts to be granted by external sources, but qualities that can be awakened and nurtured from within. The Tin Woodman's journey teaches us that it is the intentions and actions of the heart that truly define our capacity for love and empathy.

Beyond his individual story, the Tin Woodman's character holds deeper philosophical meaning. He highlights the importance of embracing vulnerability, as it is through vulnerability that we open ourselves up to love and connection. His journey reminds us that it is in our relationships and emotional bonds that we find purpose, fulfillment, and a sense of belonging.

Moreover, the Tin Woodman's story encourages us to reflect on our own search for love and compassion. It invites us to examine the barriers we may have built around our hearts and to recognize the transformative power of emotional connection in our lives. By embracing our own capacity for love and empathy, we can create meaningful connections with others and contribute to a more compassionate and harmonious world.

In conclusion, the character of the Tin Woodman in "The Wizard of Oz" is a testament to the universal longing for love and compassion. His journey reminds us that true strength and goodness come from within, and that the heart is the source of our capacity for empathy and connection. Through his story, we are inspired to embrace our own vulnerability, nurture our capacity for love, and foster meaningful relationships that bring fulfillment and purpose to our lives.

The Scarecrow

The Scarecrow is a beloved character in "The Wizard of Oz" who captivates readers and viewers with his endearing personality, inspiring journey, and profound insights into the nature of intelligence. Made entirely of straw, the Scarecrow initially believes that he lacks a brain and yearns for the gift of intelligence. However, as the story unfolds, the Scarecrow's true wisdom and intellectual capabilities are revealed, challenging the notion that intelligence is solely determined by physical attributes.

Throughout the story, the Scarecrow consistently displays remarkable problem-solving skills, quick thinking, and logical reasoning. Despite his perceived lack of a brain, he consistently comes up with clever ideas and solutions to the challenges that he and his companions face on their journey. From devising a plan to cross a treacherous field of poppies to outsmarting the Wicked Witch of the West, the Scarecrow's intelligence shines through his actions.

The Scarecrow's journey teaches us that true intelligence is not dependent on physical characteristics but is instead a product of experience, critical thinking skills, and the ability to adapt and learn. He demonstrates that knowledge and wisdom can be gained through observation, curiosity, and an open mind. The Scarecrow's willingness to question assumptions and explore new ideas allows him to overcome obstacles and contribute valuable insights to the group.

Furthermore, the Scarecrow's character challenges the stereotype that intelligence is limited to formal education. Despite not having a formal education, the Scarecrow possesses an innate intellectual capacity that is nurtured through his experiences and interactions. His desire to learn and grow serves as a reminder that intelligence is not confined to the classroom but can be cultivated through real-life experiences and a thirst for knowledge.

Additionally, the Scarecrow's intelligence is complemented by his kind-heartedness and empathy towards others. He consistently demonstrates compassion and empathy, offering support and encouragement to his companions and those they encounter on their journey. His ability to understand and connect with others on an emotional level highlights the importance of emotional intelligence and the role it plays in our interactions and relationships.

In addition to his intellectual prowess, the Scarecrow embodies the power of imagination and creativity. He uses his vivid imagination to envision possibilities and explore new ideas. His creative thinking allows him to see beyond the limitations of his physical form and envision a life filled with possibilities. The Scarecrow's ability to think outside the box and embrace unconventional ideas challenges the notion of intelligence as a rigid and fixed concept.

Moreover, the Scarecrow's character arc represents the transformative nature of intelligence. As he embarks on his journey, he gradually realizes that true intelligence is not something that can be given or acquired externally but is a quality that resides within oneself. Through his experiences and interactions, the Scarecrow learns that intelligence is not defined by physical attributes, but by the ability to think critically, adapt to new situations, and embrace the power of knowledge.

In conclusion, the Scarecrow in "The Wizard of Oz" is a character that challenges conventional notions of intelligence. Despite his physical appearance and initial belief that he lacks a brain, the Scarecrow proves time and again that true intelligence comes from experience, critical thinking, and the ability to adapt and learn. His journey serves as a powerful reminder that intelligence is not limited to physical attributes or formal education, but is a product of curiosity, imagination, empathy, and the willingness to question and explore. The Scarecrow's story inspires us to embrace our own intellectual potential and recognize the multifaceted nature of intelligence in all its forms.

Humans in nature

Humans and nature share a profound and intricate relationship that spans across our existence. From the early days of our evolution to the present, nature has played a vital role in shaping our physical, mental, and emotional well-being.

At a fundamental level, humans are a part of nature. Our bodies are intricately connected to the natural world, and we rely on its resources for our survival and sustenance. Our physiological systems are finely tuned to interact with the environment, from the way our skin responds to sunlight to the way our lungs absorb oxygen from the air. We are deeply intertwined with the natural world, and our health and vitality depend on its equilibrium.

Beyond our physical connection, nature has a profound impact on our mental and emotional well-being. Countless studies have shown that spending time in nature has a positive effect on our mood, reducing stress, anxiety, and depression. The sights, sounds, and smells of nature have a calming and soothing effect on our nervous system, helping to restore balance and promote a sense of tranquility. Whether it's walking through a forest, listening to the sound of waves crashing on the shore, or watching a sunset, these experiences in nature bring us a sense of peace and serenity.

Nature also has a remarkable ability to inspire and awaken our senses. The beauty and diversity of the natural world can ignite our imagination and stimulate our creativity. The intricate patterns of a blooming flower, the symphony of birdsong in the early morning, or the vibrant colors of a sunset can all spark a sense of wonder and awe. These experiences of awe can expand our perspective, open our minds to new possibilities, and fuel our creative endeavors.

Additionally, nature provides us with a sense of connection and belonging. When we immerse ourselves in natural environments, we become aware of our place within the larger web of life. We see ourselves as part of a vast and interconnected ecosystem, where every living organism has a role to play. This awareness fosters a sense of humility and reverence for the natural world, reminding us of our responsibility to protect and preserve it.

Furthermore, our connection to nature can inspire us to adopt more sustainable and environmentally-friendly practices. When we witness the beauty and fragility of the natural world, we develop a deep sense of respect and gratitude. We understand the importance of conserving resources, reducing waste, and treading lightly on the Earth. Our connection to nature encourages us to be mindful of our actions, making choices that align with ecological sustainability.

In today's fast-paced and technology-driven world, it is easy to become disconnected from nature. However, nurturing our relationship with the natural world is essential for our well-being and the well-being of the planet. Whether it's taking a hike in the mountains, gardening in our backyard, or simply sitting under a tree, finding ways to connect with nature can bring us a sense of grounding, healing, and rejuvenation.

In conclusion, the connection between humans and nature is deep-rooted and multifaceted. Nature provides us with physical nourishment, mental restoration, emotional well-being, and a sense of connection and purpose. As we navigate the complexities of modern life, it is crucial to prioritize and nurture our relationship with the natural world. By doing so, we not only enhance our own well-being but also contribute to the preservation and sustainability of the planet we call home.

Bioelectric

Life is an extraordinary tapestry woven with the threads of bioelectricity, an intricate and pervasive force that permeates every aspect of biological existence. From the microscopic realm of individual cells to the grand symphony of complex multicellular organisms, bioelectricity serves as the fundamental conductor orchestrating the harmonious functioning of life itself.

At its core, bioelectricity encompasses the electrical phenomena and processes that occur within living organisms. It encompasses the intricate electrical signals, currents, and potentials that traverse the intricate networks of cells, tissues, and organs. These bioelectrical processes are the fundamental building blocks underlying the myriad of biological functions that sustain life and enable its intricate dance.

At the cellular level, bioelectricity plays a profound role in cell signaling and communication. Cells generate and transmit electrical signals, known as action potentials, to convey information and instructions to neighboring cells. These electrical impulses serve as the language of cellular communication, enabling cells to coordinate and synchronize their activities. Through this complex network of bioelectrical communication, cells orchestrate vital processes, including growth, development, differentiation, and response to external stimuli.

Bioelectricity also forms the foundation of the intricate and awe-inspiring workings of the nervous system. Neurons, the specialized cells of the nervous system, rely on electrical impulses to transmit information throughout the body. These electrical signals, generated by the movement of ions across neuronal membranes, allow for the rapid and precise transmission of information. They enable us to perceive the world around us, process sensory stimuli, engage in cognitive processes, and execute intricate motor actions. The bioelectricity of the nervous system is what allows us to experience the richness of our thoughts, memories, and emotions, forming the very essence of our consciousness.

Moreover, bioelectricity is intricately intertwined with the functioning of the cardiovascular system, ensuring the steady rhythm that sustains life. The heart, a remarkable organ of bioelectrical coordination, relies on precise electrical signals for its rhythmic contractions. Specialized cells within the heart generate electrical impulses that propagate through the cardiac muscle, coordinating the synchronized contraction of its chambers. The bioelectricity of the heart ensures the efficient pumping of blood, delivering vital oxygen and nutrients to every tissue and organ, while removing waste products from the body.

Beyond these vital systems, bioelectricity plays a role in numerous other physiological processes. It contributes to the contraction of muscles, allowing for movement and physical activity. Bioelectrical signals also regulate the peristaltic movement of the digestive system, facilitating the breakdown and absorption of nutrients. Furthermore, bioelectricity is involved in processes such as wound healing, tissue regeneration, and immune responses, where electrical signals guide cellular migration, proliferation, and differentiation, promoting the body's ability to repair and restore itself.

Understanding and harnessing the power of bioelectricity have profound implications in the realm of medicine. Electrical stimulation techniques, such as transcutaneous electrical nerve stimulation (TENS) and neuromodulation, are employed to manage pain, alleviate symptoms of neurological disorders, and promote healing. Implantable bioelectric devices, such as pacemakers, defibrillators, and deep brain stimulators, interface with the body's bioelectrical systems to restore or regulate normal physiological functions. The field of bioelectrics holds immense promise for the development of innovative therapies and interventions, offering new avenues for the treatment of various diseases and conditions.

In conclusion, bioelectricity is the invisible force that underpins the intricate dance of life. It forms the foundation of cellular communication, enables the marvelous complexities of the nervous system, sustains the rhythmic beating of the heart, and governs a multitude of physiological processes that ensure the thriving of organisms. By unraveling its mysteries and harnessing its power, researchers and healthcare professionals can unlock new frontiers in medicine, enhance our understanding of life's profound intricacies, and improve the well-being of individuals and the world we inhabit.

String Theory

String theory is a deeply intricate and captivating field of study that has revolutionized our understanding of the fundamental nature of the universe. It is a theoretical framework that goes beyond the traditional view of particles as point-like objects, proposing that the fundamental building blocks of reality are tiny, vibrating strings of energy. These strings, which exist in multiple dimensions, give rise to the rich tapestry of particles and forces that govern the cosmos.

At its core, string theory suggests that the properties of particles, such as their mass, charge, and spin, arise from the various ways in which the strings vibrate. Just as the different harmonics produced by a vibrating guitar string give rise to distinct musical notes, the different vibrational modes of the strings in string theory correspond to different particles in the universe. This remarkable feature of string theory provides a unified framework that encompasses all known particles and their interactions, including the elusive force of gravity.

One of the most intriguing aspects of string theory is its potential to reconcile the seemingly incompatible theories of quantum mechanics and general relativity. Quantum mechanics describes the behavior of particles on small scales, where probabilistic phenomena and wave-particle duality are fundamental. On the other hand, general relativity describes the force of gravity and the curvature of spacetime on cosmic scales. These two theories have been incredibly successful at their respective scales, but their combination has proven to be a formidable challenge. String theory offers a promising avenue for unification by providing a consistent mathematical description that encompasses both quantum mechanics and general relativity.

In addition to its unifying potential, string theory also predicts the existence of extra dimensions beyond the familiar three spatial dimensions and one time dimension. These additional dimensions, often referred to as "compactified" dimensions, are curled up on scales much smaller than we can currently observe. While these compactified dimensions may seem abstract and difficult to comprehend, they play a crucial role in shaping the properties of particles and the forces they interact with. The existence of these extra dimensions has profound implications for our understanding of gravity, particle physics, and the nature of spacetime itself.

Furthermore, string theory has deep connections to other branches of physics, mathematics, and even philosophy. It has influenced diverse areas such as black hole physics, cosmology, quantum field theory, and the study of condensed matter systems. In fact, ideas from string theory have led to breakthroughs in seemingly unrelated fields, providing new insights and opening up new avenues of research.

However, it is important to note that string theory is still a subject of active research and debate. Many of its predictions lie beyond the reach of current experimental techniques, making it difficult to directly test the theory. Additionally, string theory is a vast and evolving field with many different variations and formulations, each with its own unique predictions and challenges. This diversity within the field has led to a rich tapestry of ideas and approaches, sparking fruitful collaborations and stimulating new lines of inquiry.

In conclusion, string theory stands as a remarkable framework that offers a profound and unified understanding of the fundamental nature of the universe. It presents a vision where vibrating strings of energy form the fabric of reality, weaving together particles, forces, and the very structure of spacetime. While the theory is still a work in progress and faces significant challenges, the exploration of string theory has already yielded remarkable insights and pushed the boundaries of our understanding. It continues to inspire scientists and ignite the imagination, leading us on a journey of discovery towards a deeper understanding of the cosmos.

The Heart of the Cosmos

"The Heart of Humans" is a captivating and thought-provoking novel written by CW Fortney that delves into the profound themes of self-discovery, the power of belief, and the importance of inner strength. Set in the enchanting land of Oz, the story follows the extraordinary journey of the main character, Dorothy, who finds herself unexpectedly transported to this magical realm and embarks on a quest to find her way back home. Throughout her adventure, Dorothy encounters various challenges, meets fascinating characters, and learns important lessons about courage, friendship, and the strength that lies within her.

While the concept of the heart of the cosmos is not explicitly explored in the book, it can be interpreted as a metaphor for the underlying interconnectedness and universal energy that permeates the story. The heart symbolizes love, compassion, and the pursuit of inner truth. It represents the driving force behind Dorothy's journey and her transformation throughout the narrative. By tapping into the power of the heart, Dorothy discovers her own agency and learns to believe in herself, ultimately leading to her self-discovery and the realization that she has the power to achieve her goals.

The heart of the cosmos can be understood as a powerful metaphor for the interconnectedness and universal energy that flows through all living beings. It represents the essence of love, compassion, and the pursuit of inner truth. In the context of "The Heart of Humans," it symbolizes the driving force behind Dorothy's journey and her transformation. By connecting with the heart of the cosmos, Dorothy taps into her own inner strength and discovers her true potential.

Throughout the story, Dorothy's encounters with various characters further emphasize the significance of the heart and its connection to the cosmos. The Tin Woodman, for example, despite his perceived lack of a physical heart, consistently demonstrates acts of kindness, empathy, and selflessness. His character serves as a powerful reminder that true strength and goodness come from within and that empathy and love have the power to transform lives.

Similarly, the Scarecrow challenges the notion that intelligence is solely determined by physical attributes. Despite initially believing that he lacks a brain, the Scarecrow consistently displays remarkable problem-solving skills, quick thinking, and logical reasoning. His journey teaches us that true intelligence is not dependent on physical characteristics but is instead a product of experience, critical thinking skills, and the ability to adapt and learn.

In addition to the individual character arcs, the heart of the cosmos also represents the underlying force that drives the characters' transformations and the interconnectedness that binds them together. It serves as a reminder that we are all connected, both to one another and to the greater universe. By embracing love, compassion, and the pursuit of inner truth, the characters in the book embark on transformative journeys of self-discovery and realize their true potential.

"The Heart of Humans" ultimately invites readers to reflect on their own journeys of self-discovery and the power of belief in shaping their lives. It encourages us to tap into the power of the heart, to listen to our inner voice, and to have faith in ourselves and our abilities. It reminds us that true strength and goodness come from within, and that by embracing love, compassion, and the pursuit of inner truth, we can achieve personal growth, make a positive impact in the world, and find our way back home.

In conclusion, "The Heart of Humans" is a captivating and inspiring novel that explores the themes of self-discovery, belief, and inner strength. While the concept of the heart of the cosmos is not explicitly discussed, it serves as a powerful metaphor for the underlying interconnectedness and universal energy that flows through the story. By embracing the power of the heart, the characters embark on transformative journeys, discover their true potential, and inspire readers to reflect on their own paths of self-discovery and the profound impact of belief in shaping their lives.

The heart of the cosmos is a perfect harmony musical the creates life. Music is a universal language that transcends cultural boundaries and speaks to the depths of our souls. It has the remarkable ability to evoke emotions, ignite our imaginations, and create a sense of unity among people from all walks of life. In the context of "The Wizard of Oz," music plays a central role in the storytelling, character development, and emotional resonance of the narrative.

One of the most iconic and beloved songs from "The Wizard of Oz" is "Over the Rainbow." This timeless ballad, sung by Judy Garland's character Dorothy, captures the essence of longing and hope. The song expresses Dorothy's desire for a place where troubles melt away and dreams come true. It speaks to the universal human longing for a better and brighter future, resonating with audiences of all ages and backgrounds. "Over the Rainbow" has become an anthem of hope and the pursuit of dreams, reminding us of the power of imagination and the possibility of a better tomorrow.

In addition to "Over the Rainbow," the film features a collection of memorable songs that contribute to the emotional journey of the characters. For example, "We're Off to See the Wizard" is a lively and infectious tune that accompanies Dorothy and her companions as they embark on their journey to find the Wizard. This song captures the excitement and anticipation of new adventures, inspiring viewers to embrace the unknown and step outside their comfort zones.

Furthermore, music in "The Wizard of Oz" serves as a means of expression and self-discovery for the characters. The Scarecrow, Tin Woodman, and Cowardly Lion each have their own solo songs that convey their desires and aspirations. The Scarecrow's song, "If I Only Had a Brain," expresses his longing for intelligence, while the Tin Woodman's "If I Only Had a Heart" reflects his desire for love and compassion. These songs highlight the characters' journey of self-realization and teach them the valuable lesson that the qualities they seek are already within them.

Moreover, the music in "The Wizard of Oz" enhances the storytelling and deepens the emotional connection between the audience and the characters. The songs create a sense of empathy and resonance, allowing viewers to share in the characters' experiences and emotions. Whether it's the joyous celebration of "Ding-Dong! The Witch is Dead" or the poignant reflection of "Somewhere Over the Rainbow," the music adds depth and richness to the narrative, immersing the audience in the magical world of Oz.

Beyond its emotional impact, the music in "The Wizard of Oz" also conveys important themes and messages. The songs explore timeless themes such as friendship, courage, and the power of belief. Through the characters' songs and their interactions with each other, the film teaches valuable lessons about the strength that comes from unity, the importance of facing fears, and the transformative power of belief in oneself. The music serves as a vehicle for conveying these messages, making them accessible and memorable to viewers of all ages.

In addition to the original songs, the musical score of "The Wizard of Oz" also plays a significant role in enhancing the film's atmosphere and guiding the audience through the story. The score, composed by Harold Arlen and Herbert Stothart, incorporates elements of fantasy, adventure, and emotion, creating a captivating and immersive sonic experience. From the whimsical melodies that accompany the journey along the Yellow Brick Road to the suspenseful cues that underscore the encounters with the Wicked Witch, the music heightens the tension, excitement, and emotional impact of the film.

Furthermore, the cultural impact of the music in "The Wizard of Oz" extends far beyond the film itself. The songs have become part of the collective consciousness, recognized and cherished by people around the world. They have been covered by countless artists, adapted into various languages, and performed in numerous stage productions and concerts. The enduring popularity of the music speaks to its timeless appeal and its ability to touch the hearts of audiences across generations.

In conclusion, music in "The Wizard of Oz" is a powerful and integral part of the film's storytelling and emotional impact. The iconic songs, such as "Over the Rainbow," "We're Off to See the Wizard," and the character solos, enhance the narrative, express the characters' desires and aspirations, and convey important themes and messages. The musical score further enhances the atmosphere and emotional resonance of the film. The music creates a deep emotional connection with the audience, making the story and its lessons resonate long after the film ends. "The Wizard of Oz" reminds us of the profound and lasting power of music to touch our hearts, inspire our dreams, and bring us together in a shared experience of joy and wonder.

"The Wizard of Oz" does not directly reference the Bible or music. However, the story emphasizes the power of belief, self-discovery, and the importance of inner strength. The teachings of Dr. Wayne Dyer, a self-help author and motivational speaker, align with the themes of the story, highlighting the power of positive thinking and belief in oneself. While the story and the teachings of Dr. Wayne Dyer do not specifically reference the Bible or music, they promote personal growth, resilience, and the ability to overcome challenges through inner strength and positive beliefs.

Musical instruments

Musical instruments are devices or tools that are used to create or produce musical sounds. They can be categorized into various types based on different criteria such as the way they produce sound, the method of playing, and the cultural or geographical origin. There is of the wide variety of musical instruments that exist. Each instrument has its own unique sound and playing technique, contributing to the rich and diverse world of music.

Music is a universal language that transcends cultural boundaries and speaks to the depths of our souls. It has the remarkable ability to evoke emotions, ignite our imaginations, and create a sense of unity among people from all walks of life. Music has been an integral part of human existence for centuries, serving a multitude of purposes and enriching our lives in countless ways.

One of the primary functions of music is its ability to evoke emotions. Whether it's a powerful symphony that stirs feelings of awe and grandeur or a gentle lullaby that soothes and comforts, music has the power to elicit a wide range of emotional responses. It can uplift our spirits, provide solace during difficult times, and serve as a form of catharsis. The emotional impact of music is undeniable, as it has the ability to touch our hearts and connect us on a deeply personal level.

Music also has the extraordinary power to bring people together. It serves as a common thread that unites individuals from different cultures, backgrounds, and walks of life. Whether it's attending a live concert, singing in a choir, or dancing to a favorite song, music has the ability to create a sense of community and foster connections. It has the unique ability to transcend language barriers, allowing people to communicate and express themselves in ways that words alone cannot. Music has the power to break down barriers and promote understanding, tolerance, and unity among diverse groups of people.

Moreover, music is a powerful form of self-expression. It provides individuals with a means to convey their thoughts, emotions, and experiences. Through songwriting, composing, or performing, artists can share their unique perspectives and stories with the world. Music allows us to express our innermost thoughts and feelings, offering a cathartic release and a way to make sense of the world around us. It serves as a platform for personal growth, self-discovery, and identity exploration.

In addition to its emotional and social impact, music has been shown to have numerous cognitive benefits. Research has demonstrated that listening to music can improve cognitive function, enhance memory, and stimulate creativity. It has the power to engage multiple areas of the brain simultaneously, creating complex neural connections and enhancing cognitive abilities. Music therapy has also been used to aid in the rehabilitation of individuals with cognitive impairments, mental health conditions, and neurological disorders. The therapeutic value of music is undeniable, as it has the ability to reduce stress, alleviate pain, and improve overall well-being.

Furthermore, music plays a significant role in cultural preservation and identity. It reflects the traditions, values, and history of different communities, serving as a repository of cultural heritage. Traditional music and folk songs are often passed down through generations, preserving the stories and traditions of a particular culture. Music helps to shape and define cultural identity, providing a sense of belonging and fostering pride in one's heritage. It also serves as a means of cultural exchange, allowing individuals to explore and appreciate the diversity of musical styles and traditions from around the world.

Beyond its individual and social impact, music has also been recognized for its therapeutic qualities. Music therapy is a recognized field that utilizes music as a means to improve physical, emotional, and mental well-being. It has been shown to reduce anxiety, promote relaxation, and enhance communication skills. Music therapy is used in a variety of settings, including hospitals, rehabilitation centers, and schools, to assist individuals in managing pain, improving motor skills, and enhancing overall quality of life.

Additionally, music has a profound impact on our daily lives and routines. It has the power to set the mood and create atmosphere in various settings, such as restaurants, stores, and social gatherings. Music can influence our energy levels, productivity, and even our perception of time. It has the ability to transport us to different places, evoke memories, and create a soundtrack for our lives.

In conclusion, music is a powerful and multifaceted art form that has a profound impact on individuals and society as a whole. It has the ability to evoke emotions, bring people together, serve as a form of self-expression, and provide cognitive and therapeutic benefits. Music enhances our experiences, influences our moods, and contributes to cultural preservation and identity. Whether it's through listening, performing, or engaging with music in various forms, we can harness the transformative power of music to enrich our lives, enhance our well-being, and build bridges of understanding and unity in an ever-changing world.

Human Heart Expressions

The art of human heart expression is a profound and multifaceted practice that encompasses a wide range of creative and emotional outlets. It is a deeply personal and introspective journey that allows individuals to delve into the depths of their innermost thoughts, feelings, and experiences, and express them through various artistic mediums.

One of the most powerful aspects of the art of human heart expression is its ability to transcend language and communicate on a universal level. Art has the unique capacity to evoke emotions, provoke thought, and elicit visceral responses from viewers or listeners. Whether it is through visual arts, music, dance, literature, or any other form of creative expression, individuals can tap into their innermost selves and communicate their deepest truths in ways that words alone often fail to capture.

Visual arts, such as painting, drawing, sculpture, and photography, offer a visual representation of the artist's inner world. Through the use of colors, shapes, textures, and composition, artists can convey their emotions, experiences, and perspectives. Each brushstroke, each line, and each choice of medium is a deliberate expression of the artist's unique vision and interpretation of the world around them. From vibrant and energetic abstract pieces to serene and contemplative landscapes, visual artists can use their chosen medium to communicate a wide range of emotions and concepts.

Music, on the other hand, has the remarkable ability to evoke emotions and create a profound emotional connection between the artist and the listener. Through melody, rhythm, harmony, and lyrics, musicians can express their deepest feelings and experiences. The power of music lies in its ability to transcend cultural and linguistic boundaries, speaking directly to the heart and soul of the listener. It has the capacity to uplift, inspire, heal, and provide solace in times of joy or sorrow. From heart-wrenching ballads that touch the depths of our emotions to soaring symphonies that fill us with awe and wonder, music has the power to transcend the limitations of words and connect us on a primal level.

Dance, as a form of human heart expression, combines movement, rhythm, and emotion to convey a story or evoke a particular mood. Through the graceful or powerful movements of the body, dancers can communicate their innermost thoughts and feelings. Dance has the capacity to transcend verbal language and convey emotions and experiences that are difficult to put into words. It allows individuals to express their individuality, celebrate their cultural heritage, and connect with others in a visceral and profound way. From the fluid and expressive movements of contemporary dance to the precise and intricate footwork of ballet, dance has the power to captivate and transport both the performer and the audience.

Literature, including poetry, prose, and storytelling, is another powerful medium for human heart expression. Through the written word, authors can delve into the depths of their imagination, explore complex emotions and experiences, and create narratives that resonate with readers on a deeply personal level. Literature has the ability to transport readers to different worlds, provoke reflection, and provide insight into the human condition. From the intimate and introspective verses of poetry to the epic and sweeping narratives of novels, literature allows individuals to explore the depths of human emotion and experience in a way that is both personal and universal.

The art of human heart expression is not limited to these specific forms of artistic expression. It can be found in theater, film, sculpture, performance art, and countless other creative outlets. Each medium offers a unique and powerful way for individuals to express their innermost thoughts, emotions, and experiences, and connect with others on a profound level.

In conclusion, the art of human heart expression is a deeply personal and transformative practice that allows individuals to communicate and share their innermost thoughts, feelings, and experiences through various artistic mediums. It is a universal language that transcends cultural and linguistic boundaries, evoking emotions, provoking thought, and fostering connections. Through art, individuals can explore their inner world, express their unique perspectives, and create a profound impact on themselves and others. Whether it is through the stroke of a brush, the strum of a guitar, the movement of a body, or the turn of a page, the art of human heart expression invites us to dive deep into the realm of our emotions and connect with the shared humanity that unites us all.

Emotions are a fundamental aspect of human experience and serve important functions in our lives. Humans have emotions because they play a crucial role in our psychological and physiological well-being. Emotions are complex and multifaceted, and their study continues to be a subject of ongoing research in fields such as psychology, neuroscience, and sociology.

One of the primary reasons why humans have emotions is for survival and adaptation. Emotions help us respond to threats and challenges in our environment. For example, fear triggers a "fight or flight" response, preparing our bodies to either confront or escape from dangerous situations. This adaptive response increases our chances of survival and has been essential throughout human evolution.

In addition to survival, emotions also play a crucial role in communication and social bonding. Emotions serve as a means of communication, allowing us to express our thoughts, feelings, and intentions to others. They help us form social bonds, build relationships, and convey empathy and understanding. For instance, happiness and laughter can create a positive and joyful atmosphere, fostering connections with others. Similarly, sadness and compassion can elicit support and comfort from those around us.

Emotions also contribute to our decision-making processes and judgment. They provide valuable information that influences our choices and actions. Emotions help us evaluate and prioritize options based on their emotional significance. For example, feelings of disgust may guide us to avoid certain foods that could potentially be harmful. Moreover, emotions can influence our perception of situations, biases, and cognitive processes, shaping the way we interpret and make sense of the world.

Furthermore, emotions play a crucial role in memory formation and retrieval. Strong emotional experiences tend to be more memorable, helping us learn from past events and make better choices in the future. Emotions can enhance our attention and focus, facilitating learning and information processing. For example, a positive emotional state can improve memory consolidation, while negative emotions can heighten our alertness and vigilance.

Apart from their functional roles, emotions contribute to our subjective experience of life. They add depth, richness, and color to our daily encounters. Emotions give us a sense of joy, love, excitement, and fulfillment, enhancing our overall well-being and quality of life. They contribute to our sense of self and identity, shaping our individual experiences and perspectives.

Moreover, emotions can have a profound impact on our physical health. Research has shown that chronic negative emotions, such as stress, anger, and sadness, can have detrimental effects on our immune system, cardiovascular health, and overall well-being. On the other hand, positive emotions, such as happiness and gratitude, have been linked to better physical health, increased longevity, and improved resilience.

It is important to note that emotions can vary greatly among individuals and cultures. The way we experience, and express emotions can be influenced by various factors, including genetics, upbringing, and societal norms. Some emotions may be universal, while others might be culturally specific. For example, while sadness and happiness are commonly experienced across cultures, the specific triggers and expressions of these emotions may vary.

In conclusion, humans have emotions because they serve vital functions in our lives. Emotions contribute to our survival, communication, decision-making, memory, physical health, and subjective experience. They help us navigate the complexities of the world, form social connections, and make sense of our own thoughts and feelings. Understanding and managing emotions is crucial for our overall well-being and can lead to personal growth, enhanced relationships, and a more fulfilling life.

The concept of God and the divine soul is a deeply profound and complex topic that has captivated human minds for millennia. It is a subject that has been explored and contemplated by philosophers, theologians, and spiritual seekers across cultures and throughout history. The questions surrounding the existence and nature of God, as well as the understanding of the divine soul, delve into the very essence of human existence and the mysteries of the universe.

God, often referred to as the supreme being, is a concept that transcends any single religion or belief system. It encompasses the idea of an all-powerful, all-knowing entity that is the ultimate source of creation and sustains the cosmos. Different religious and spiritual traditions have various names, descriptions, and understandings of God. For some, God is seen as a personal deity with anthropomorphic qualities, while for others, God is perceived as an abstract force or energy beyond human comprehension. The concept of God is deeply intertwined with notions of divinity, transcendence, and the cosmic order.

The divine soul, also known as the inner self or higher self, is often described as the spiritual essence that resides within each individual. It is believed to be the part of human beings that connects them to the divine and carries within it the potential for spiritual growth, wisdom, and enlightenment. The divine soul is said to be eternal and unchanging, transcending the limitations of the physical body and existing beyond the boundaries of time and space. It is often seen as the seat of consciousness and the source of inner guidance, intuition, and moral discernment.

Belief in God and the concept of the divine soul can provide individuals with a sense of purpose, meaning, and direction in life. It offers a framework for understanding the mysteries of the universe and the human experience. The belief in a higher power can bring comfort, solace, and a sense of belonging, as individuals find solace in the knowledge that they are part of something greater than themselves. The divine soul, seen as the divine spark within each person, serves as a source of inspiration, strength, and inner wisdom.

Furthermore, belief in God and the divine soul often plays a significant role in shaping moral frameworks and ethical values. Many religious and spiritual traditions emphasize the importance of living in alignment with divine principles such as love, compassion, justice, and forgiveness. The belief in the divine soul encourages individuals to cultivate these qualities and to strive for personal growth and spiritual development. It serves as a guiding force in making decisions, treating others with kindness and respect, and contributing to the well-being of the world.

However, it is important to recognize that beliefs about God and the divine soul can vary widely among individuals and cultures. Different religious traditions have their own unique teachings and interpretations of these concepts. Moreover, personal experiences, cultural backgrounds, and individual journeys of spiritual exploration can shape and influence one's understanding of God and the divine soul. It is essential to approach discussions about these topics with openness, respect, and a willingness to learn from different perspectives.

In conclusion, the concept of God and the divine soul is a deeply intricate and multifaceted subject that has captivated human beings throughout history. Belief in a higher power and the existence of a divine soul can provide individuals with a sense of purpose, meaning, and connection to something greater than themselves. It serves as a source of inspiration, moral guidance, and inner wisdom. While beliefs about God and the divine soul may differ among individuals and cultures, engaging in thoughtful and respectful dialogue can deepen our understanding of the human experience and foster a greater appreciation for the diversity of spiritual perspectives in the world.

Healing the Heart

Healing the heart is a deeply transformative and multifaceted process that involves addressing emotional wounds, releasing past hurts, and nurturing oneself with love and compassion. It is a profound journey of self-discovery and growth that can lead to profound personal transformation and a renewed sense of well-being.

The journey of healing the heart begins with self-reflection and self-awareness. It requires individuals to delve deep within themselves, exploring their past experiences, traumas, and patterns of behavior. This process allows individuals to gain a deeper understanding of their emotional wounds and how they have impacted their lives. By shining a light on these wounds, individuals can begin the process of healing and transformation.

Forgiveness is a critical aspect of healing the heart. It involves letting go of resentment, anger, and blame towards oneself and others. Forgiveness is not about condoning or forgetting past hurts, but rather about releasing the emotional burden associated with them. It is a powerful act of self-compassion and liberation that allows individuals to free themselves from the weight of the past and create space for healing and growth.

In addition to forgiveness, healing the heart requires individuals to cultivate self-compassion and self-love. It involves treating oneself with kindness, understanding, and acceptance, even in the face of past mistakes or perceived shortcomings. Self-compassion means recognizing one's inherent worth and embracing oneself with unconditional love and care. By nurturing a compassionate relationship with oneself, individuals can create a foundation of self-acceptance and self-worth, essential for healing and personal growth.

Healing the heart also involves exploring and processing emotions. It requires individuals to allow themselves to fully experience and express their feelings, even if they are uncomfortable or painful. By acknowledging and honoring their emotions, individuals can release pent-up energy and find a sense of release. This process allows for emotional healing and creates space for new growth and possibilities.

Moreover, healing the heart often involves seeking support from trusted friends, family, or professionals. Sharing one's feelings and experiences with others can provide a safe and supportive space for healing and growth. It allows individuals to feel seen, heard, and validated, which can be incredibly healing. Seeking professional help, such as therapy or counseling, can offer additional guidance and support in the healing process.

In the journey of healing the heart, it is essential to cultivate practices of self-care and self-nurturing. This includes engaging in activities that bring joy, relaxation, and nourishment to the mind, body, and soul. Self-care practices can vary for each individual, but may include activities such as meditation, yoga, spending time in nature, reading, or engaging in creative pursuits. By prioritizing self-care, individuals can replenish their energy and create a supportive environment for healing and growth.

Furthermore, healing the heart often involves reevaluating and shifting one's mindset and beliefs. Negative self-talk and limiting beliefs can keep individuals stuck in patterns of pain and self-sabotage. By cultivating a mindset of self-compassion, self-belief, and optimism, individuals can break free from these patterns and create a positive and empowering narrative for their lives. Affirmations, positive self-talk, and cognitive restructuring techniques can support this shift in mindset.

Additionally, engaging in acts of kindness and service can be instrumental in healing the heart. By extending love, compassion, and support to others, individuals create a ripple effect of healing and positivity. Acts of kindness can range from small gestures of generosity to larger-scale efforts to make a difference in the world. Engaging in acts of service can provide a sense of purpose and fulfillment, fostering healing and growth within oneself and the community.

Moreover, exploring and connecting with spirituality can play a significant role in healing the heart. Spirituality can provide individuals with a sense of purpose, meaning, and connection to something greater than themselves. It can involve practices such as prayer, meditation, or engaging with religious or philosophical teachings. By deepening their spiritual connection, individuals can find solace, guidance, and strength in their healing journey.

Additionally, integrating practices that promote physical well-being can contribute to the healing of the heart. Engaging in regular exercise, eating a balanced and nutritious diet, and getting sufficient rest and sleep are essential for overall well-being and can have a positive impact on emotional healing. Physical activities such as yoga, dance, or hiking can not only strengthen the body but also promote relaxation and the release of emotional tension.

Furthermore, engaging in practices that promote personal growth and self-discovery can enhance the healing of the heart. This may involve reading books or attending workshops that offer insights and tools for personal development. It can also include exploring new hobbies, learning new skills, or engaging in creative outlets that foster self-expression and self-discovery. By continuously seeking opportunities for growth and self-improvement, individuals can deepen their healing journey and create a life of fulfillment and purpose.

Ultimately, the journey of healing the heart is a lifelong process. It requires dedication, patience, and self-compassion. Each individual's path to healing will be unique, influenced by their experiences, beliefs, and personal growth. It is important to approach this journey with openness, curiosity, and a willingness to learn and grow. By embarking on the journey of healing the heart, individuals can create profound transformation in their lives, fostering greater peace, joy, and fulfillment.

In conclusion, healing the heart is a multifaceted and deeply transformative journey that involves self-reflection, forgiveness, self-compassion, emotional exploration, seeking support, self-care, mindset shifts, acts of kindness, spiritual connection, physical well-being, personal growth, and a lifelong commitment to self-discovery and healing. By embracing this journey, individuals can heal emotional wounds, cultivate self-acceptance and love, and create a life filled with greater peace, joy, and fulfillment.

The Human Heart

The human heart, a marvel of biological engineering, stands as a testament to the miracles of life and the intricacies of our existence. Nestled within the protective confines of the chest, this remarkable organ beats tirelessly, orchestrating the symphony of life by pumping oxygen-rich blood to every cell in the body. Yet, beyond its physical attributes, the heart carries within it a profound tapestry of symbolism, representing love, emotions, resilience, courage, interconnectedness, and the very essence of our humanity.

At its core, the heart is an emblem of love, the universal language that knows no bounds. It is the heart that flutters with excitement when we experience the exhilaration of new love, the heart that aches with longing when we are separated from our loved ones, and the heart that overflows with tenderness and compassion in moments of connection. The heart is a symbol of the boundless capacity for love that resides within us, reminding us of the transformative power of this profound emotion.

Emotions, the vibrant brushstrokes of our inner lives, find their home within the chambers of the heart. It is the heart that races with anticipation, the heart that sinks with sorrow, and the heart that swells with joy. From the depths of despair to the heights of ecstasy, the heart serves as a vessel that carries the full spectrum of human emotions, reminding us of the depth and richness of our inner world. It is through our emotions that we connect with others, experience the world, and find meaning in our existence.

Courage, an attribute that resides within the heart, empowers us to face adversity, overcome challenges, and embrace growth. It is the heart that beats with unwavering determination, urging us to step outside our comfort zones, pursue our dreams, and confront our fears. The heart serves as a symbol of resilience and strength, reminding us of our innate ability to persevere and find inner fortitude even in the face of the most daunting obstacles.

Symbolically, the heart represents the seat of the soul, the center of our spiritual essence. It is believed to be the source of our intuition, inner wisdom, and connection to the divine. The heart invites us to listen to its whispers, guiding us on our spiritual journey and aligning us with our true purpose. By following the path of the heart, we can tap into our deepest truths, experience profound spiritual growth, and cultivate a sense of peace and fulfillment.

Metaphorically, the heart represents vulnerability and emotional openness. Opening our hearts requires us to embrace our true selves, including our fears, insecurities, and imperfections. It is through vulnerability that we forge deep connections with others, cultivate empathy and compassion, and experience genuine intimacy. The heart invites us to remove the armor of protection we may have built around ourselves, allowing us to authentically engage with the world and fully express our emotions.

Moreover, the heart serves as a powerful symbol of interconnectedness and unity. It transcends the boundaries of culture, language, and nationality, reminding us that beneath our external differences, we are all connected by the shared experience of being human. The rhythm of each individual heart resonates with the collective pulse of humanity, reinforcing our inherent interconnectedness and calling us to treat one another with kindness, empathy, and respect.

In the realms of art, literature, and music, the heart has long been a muse, inspiring countless works that explore its depths of symbolism. Artists, poets, and musicians have sought to capture the essence of the heart's symbolism, its depth of emotion, and its transformative power. Through their creations, they have delved into the profound human experience, delving into themes of love, longing, joy, and the search for meaning and connection.

In conclusion, the human heart is not simply an organ that sustains life—it is a profound symbol that encompasses the breadth of our human experience. It is a beacon of love, a wellspring of emotions, a stronghold of courage, and a reminder of our interconnectedness. The heart invites us to embrace vulnerability, cultivate compassion, and live with a deep sense of purpose and interconnectedness. It is a testament to the beauty and complexity of our shared humanity, reminding us of the infinite capacity for love and connection that defines our existence.

[The following dialogue expansion is an excerpt from a work by Melville Stewart.]

Dialogue Expansion: Free Will and Determinism

This dialogue expands on the discussion of free will and determinism from the original work by Melville Stewart. The dialogue takes place between four characters: Pelagius, Augustine, John Calvin, and Jacobus Arminius. They are gathered at the Cafe de Flore in Paris, on the eve of a conference on predestination.

Pelagius: Isn't it curious that despite our differences, we are all drawn to the same dining experience, service, and atmosphere?

Augustine: Pelagius, our inclination towards the Cafe de Flore is only part of the equation. It was our destiny to be here, together, at this moment in time.

John Calvin: I beg to differ. We cannot forget the role of the highest power. If it hadn't been decreed, none of us would be here.

Jacobus Arminius: How can you say that? Did we not all choose to come here and take each step that brought us here?

Pelagius: Indeed, we all made the choice to be here. And we can leave at any time if we wish.

Augustine: True, we have the freedom to leave, but that doesn't mean we are destined to.

John Calvin: I do not believe we are destined to leave, especially when there is much to be learned from our gathering.

Jacobus Arminius: We freely choose to sit and discuss these matters. Our destiny is not random; we have shaped it.

Pelagius: But how free are we really? Are we not all here for the same reasons? Our moral obligations have brought us together.

Augustine: On that, I partially agree with you. While we may be predetermined, we still have moral responsibilities.

John Calvin: Such beliefs defy logic. Determinism and free will are incompatible. Every event has a cause, and human actions are events. Therefore, every human action is caused.

Jacobus Arminius: That is taking assumptions too far. Every human being has the freedom to deliberate and make choices. Our actions flow from our free deliberations.

Pelagius: Right and wrong are determined by God. We have been imbued with His nature, and we know what He wills as right and wrong. We can freely choose accordingly.

Augustine: I almost agree with you, almost. A person's conscience, influenced by their beliefs, may guide them towards right or wrong.

John Calvin: Regardless of our beliefs, we were all destined to meet here and will be destined after we leave. That is the bottom line.

Jacobus Arminius: We are all entitled to our opinions and beliefs. I agree.

Pelagius: Well, in my opinion, this food smells great, and I'm sure we can all agree that it is time to eat.

Augustine: I can agree with that.

[End of Dialogue Expansion]

Note: This dialogue expansion is based on the original work by Melville Stewart and explores the themes of free will and determinism through the perspectives of the four characters.

References:

- Stewart, Melville. (Publication Year). Title of Original Work.

- Pojman, Louis. (2006). Philosophy: The Pursuit of Wisdom.
- Rauhut, Nils. (2006). Ultimate Questions.
- Seligman, M.E.P. (2002). Authentic Happiness.

Authentic Happiness is a concept introduced by positive psychologist Martin Seligman that has revolutionized the field of psychology and our understanding of well-being. It offers a comprehensive framework for achieving true happiness and fulfillment in life, going beyond the conventional notion of happiness as a fleeting emotion or a result of external circumstances. Instead, authentic happiness emphasizes the cultivation of positive emotions, engagement in meaningful activities, development of personal strengths, and the formation of deep and meaningful relationships.

At the core of authentic happiness is the recognition that happiness is not solely determined by external factors such as wealth, status, or material possessions. While these things may provide temporary pleasure or satisfaction, they are not the foundation of lasting happiness. Instead, authentic happiness emphasizes the importance of cultivating positive emotions, such as joy, gratitude, love, and contentment, which have a profound impact on our overall well-being and life satisfaction.

Positive emotions not only contribute to our subjective experience of happiness but also have far-reaching effects on our physical health, mental resilience, and overall quality of life. When we cultivate positive emotions, we are better equipped to navigate life's challenges, bounce back from setbacks, and maintain a sense of optimism and well-being. Moreover, positive emotions broaden our perspective, enhance our creativity and problem-solving abilities, and strengthen our relationships with others.

Another key aspect of authentic happiness is engagement in meaningful activities. Seligman suggests that true happiness stems from being fully absorbed and immersed in activities that align with our values, passions, and interests. When we engage in activities that are personally meaningful, we experience a state of flow, where time seems to vanish, and we are fully present and absorbed in the task at hand. This state of flow not only brings us joy and fulfillment, but it also allows us to tap into our strengths and talents, leading to a sense of accomplishment and personal growth.

Moreover, authentic happiness emphasizes the development and utilization of personal strengths. Seligman argues that each individual possesses unique strengths and talents that, when identified and nurtured, can contribute to a sense of purpose, meaning, and fulfillment in life. By identifying our strengths, whether they are in the realm of creativity, leadership, kindness, or perseverance, we can leverage them to achieve our goals, overcome challenges, and make a positive impact in the world.

In addition to cultivating positive emotions, engaging in meaningful activities, and utilizing personal strengths, authentic happiness places a strong emphasis on the formation of deep and meaningful relationships. Positive social connections and strong interpersonal bonds are essential for our well-being and happiness. By investing time and effort in building and nurturing relationships with family, friends, and the broader community, we not only experience a sense of belonging and support but also contribute to the well-being of others.

Authentic happiness also encourages individuals to seek out and prioritize experiences rather than material possessions. Research has shown that experiences, such as travel, outdoor adventures, and engaging in new activities, have a more lasting impact on our happiness and well-being than the accumulation of material possessions. By savoring and cherishing experiences, we create memories and moments that bring us joy and fulfillment throughout our lives.

In summary, authentic happiness is a multifaceted approach to well-being that encompasses various dimensions of our lives. It involves cultivating positive emotions, engaging in meaningful activities, developing personal strengths, fostering deep and meaningful relationships, and prioritizing experiences over material possessions. By embracing the principles of authentic happiness, we can embark on a transformative journey towards lasting happiness, fulfillment, and a meaningful life.

Desires

Desires are profound and intricate facets of the human psyche, intricately woven into the tapestry of our thoughts, emotions, and aspirations. They are the driving forces that propel us forward, inspiring us to dream, set goals, and take action in pursuit of a life that resonates with our deepest longings.

At the core of desires lies the innate human quest for happiness and fulfillment. We yearn for experiences, achievements, and relationships that bring us joy, contentment, and a sense of purpose. These desires may manifest in various forms, such as the desire for a loving and supportive partnership, a meaningful and fulfilling career, financial abundance, good health, or the pursuit of personal growth and self-actualization. They are the fuel that ignites our passion, motivates us to overcome obstacles, and compels us to embark on a journey of self-discovery and self-fulfillment.

Desires can also be influenced by external factors, shaping our aspirations and molding our sense of what is desirable. Society, culture, and the media play a significant role in shaping our desires by promoting certain ideals, values, and perceptions of success. These external influences can impact the way we perceive ourselves and others, influencing our desires for material possessions, social status, or recognition. It is important to critically examine these external influences and ensure that our desires are authentic expressions of our true selves, rather than mere reflections of societal expectations.

Moreover, desires encompass not only tangible outcomes but also intangible aspects of life. Many individuals harbor a yearning for personal growth, self-improvement, and the pursuit of knowledge and wisdom. These desires propel us to expand our horizons, challenge our limits, and seek opportunities for learning, acquiring new skills, and cultivating our talents. The desire for personal growth is rooted in a deep curiosity about the world and our place in it, driving us to continuously evolve, develop, and reach our full potential.

In addition to personal growth, desires often revolve around the pursuit of meaningful and authentic relationships. Human beings are inherently social creatures, wired for connection and companionship. The desire for love, intimacy, and deep connections with others drives us to seek meaningful friendships, romantic partnerships, and a sense of community. These desires for connection provide us with support, understanding, and a sense of belonging, enriching our lives and contributing to our overall well-being.

Spiritual desires also hold a significant place in the realm of human longing. Many individuals possess a deep yearning for spiritual connection, seeking a sense of transcendence, purpose, and meaning. These desires may manifest in different ways, such as engaging in spiritual practices, exploring philosophical or religious teachings, or embarking on a journey of self-discovery and inner transformation. Spiritual desires provide a framework for navigating life's challenges, offering solace, guidance, and a deep connection to something greater than ourselves.

Desires are not static but rather dynamic and ever-evolving. They can change shape, intensity, and focus as we progress through different stages of life, encounter new experiences, and gain insights into our true selves. What may have been a burning desire in our youth may give way to new aspirations and goals as we mature and gain wisdom. Our desires are shaped by our personal growth, evolving priorities, and shifting perspectives.

It is crucial to acknowledge and embrace our desires, as they serve as a compass, guiding us on our personal journey of self-discovery and fulfillment. However, it is also important to cultivate a sense of balance and discernment in our desires. While desires can be powerful motivators, it is vital to ensure that they align with our values, well-being, and the greater good. Balancing the pursuit of desires with a sense of contentment and gratitude for what we have can lead to a deeper sense of inner peace, harmony, and fulfillment.

In conclusion, desires are profound and intricate elements of the human experience. They encompass a wide spectrum of aspirations, including personal happiness, growth, meaningful connections, and spiritual fulfillment. Understanding and embracing our desires empower us to shape our lives, make choices that align with our authentic selves, and embark on a journey of self-discovery and personal growth. By cultivating a deep awareness of our desires and embracing them with intention and authenticity, we can navigate life's complexities, find fulfillment, and create a life that resonates with our truest aspirations.

True positive qualities such as kindness, empathy, and genuine connections with others are essential. These qualities are portrayed as essential for personal growth and self-discovery. The text suggests that nurturing and protecting the love within oneself and extending it to others is a positive desire, while selfishness and harmful intentions are considered negative desires.

Highlight the importance of positive qualities such as kindness, empathy, and genuine connections with others. These qualities are portrayed as essential for personal growth and self-discovery. The text suggests that nurturing and protecting the love within oneself and extending it to others is a positive desire, while selfishness and harmful intentions are considered negative desires.

Integrity

Integrity is a fundamental and multifaceted virtue that plays a crucial role in shaping individuals, relationships, organizations, and societies. It encompasses a wide range of qualities and behaviors that contribute to ethical conduct, personal growth, and the betterment of the collective.

At its core, integrity is about living in alignment with one's values and principles. It involves consistently acting in accordance with what one believes to be right and just, even when faced with challenges or temptations. Individuals with integrity possess a strong moral compass and demonstrate unwavering adherence to ethical standards.

One of the key aspects of integrity is honesty. Honest individuals are truthful in their words, actions, and interactions. They prioritize transparency and avoid deception or manipulation. By embodying honesty, individuals build trust with others, creating a foundation of openness and authenticity in their relationships.

Integrity also encompasses reliability and dependability. Individuals with integrity fulfill their commitments and obligations, demonstrating a strong sense of responsibility. They can be counted on to follow through on their promises, meet deadlines, and deliver on their commitments. Their reliability fosters trust and confidence in their capabilities.

Another important dimension of integrity is fairness and justice. Individuals with integrity treat others with respect and equity, regardless of their differences or positions of power. They advocate for fairness and strive to ensure that everyone is given equal opportunities and treated justly. Their commitment to fairness promotes a sense of equality and fosters a harmonious and inclusive environment.

Integrity also involves accountability. Individuals with integrity take ownership of their actions and accept responsibility for the consequences. They do not shy away from admitting mistakes or acknowledging when they have acted inappropriately. Instead, they learn from their errors and take steps to make amends or rectify the situation. Their accountability demonstrates humility and a commitment to personal growth.

Moreover, integrity extends beyond individual conduct to encompass ethical leadership. Leaders with integrity serve as role models and inspire others through their ethical behavior and decision-making. They prioritize the well-being of their team members, act with integrity in all aspects of their leadership, and create a culture of trust, respect, and accountability.

In organizations, integrity is a cornerstone of ethical governance and responsible business practices. Companies that prioritize integrity establish codes of conduct, ethics committees, and mechanisms for reporting unethical behavior. They promote a culture of integrity that permeates all levels of the organization, ensuring that ethical considerations inform decision-making processes.

On a societal level, integrity contributes to the creation of a just and ethical community. When individuals collectively embody integrity, they foster a culture of trust, fairness, and accountability. This, in turn, leads to a more harmonious and equitable society where individuals can thrive and contribute to the greater good.

In conclusion, integrity is a multifaceted virtue that encompasses honesty, reliability, fairness, accountability, and ethical leadership. It is about living in alignment with one's values and principles, consistently acting in accordance with ethical standards, and promoting a culture of trust, respect, and accountability. Integrity plays a vital role in personal growth, strong relationships, ethical governance, and the development of a just society. By embodying integrity, individuals and institutions contribute to a better world and foster a sense of collective well-being.

The Golden Heart

The concept of the divine heart of goodness is a profound and illuminating belief that holds the power to shape our lives and transform our understanding of ourselves and the world around us. It invites us to embark on a journey of self-discovery, exploring the depths of our being to uncover the divine essence that resides within each and every one of us.

At its core, the divine heart of goodness represents the highest expression of our true nature. It is the divine spark that ignites the flame of love, compassion, and wisdom within us. This divine essence is believed to be the source of our moral values, ethical principles, and the guiding force behind our thoughts, emotions, and actions.

When we connect with our divine heart of goodness, we tap into a wellspring of infinite love and boundless wisdom. It is through this connection that we are able to transcend the limitations of the ego and embrace the fundamental truth that we are all interconnected, part of a greater cosmic tapestry.

The divine heart of goodness inspires us to embody the highest virtues and qualities of our human potential. It calls upon us to cultivate compassion, empathy, and understanding, seeking to alleviate the suffering of others and promote their well-being. By nurturing these qualities within ourselves, we become vessels of divine love and channels of divine wisdom, radiating positivity and making a profound impact in the world.

Moreover, the recognition of the divine heart of goodness within ourselves and others forms the foundation for ethical behavior and the pursuit of justice, equality, and peace. When we honor this divine essence, we naturally strive to treat others with respect, fairness, and kindness. We recognize the inherent worth and dignity of every individual, transcending boundaries of race, gender, religion, or nationality.

The concept of the divine heart of goodness finds resonance in various spiritual and religious traditions. It is often associated with the belief in the inherent divinity of every individual, reflecting the idea that we are spiritual beings having a human experience. Through practices such as meditation, prayer, and self-reflection, individuals seek to connect with this divine essence and align their thoughts, emotions, and actions with its guiding principles.

In embracing the divine heart of goodness, we embark on a transformative journey of self-discovery and spiritual growth. We cultivate a deep sense of inner peace, harmony, and fulfillment as we align ourselves with the highest expressions of love and compassion. This alignment allows us to live a life of purpose, authenticity, and service to others, making a positive impact on the world around us.

Furthermore, the divine heart of goodness invites us to expand our understanding of love and compassion beyond ourselves and extend it to all beings and the natural world. It encourages us to recognize our interconnectedness with all of creation and to act as stewards of the Earth, caring for and honoring the planet that sustains us. By embracing an ecological consciousness, we can contribute to the healing and preservation of the environment, ensuring a sustainable future for generations to come.

In conclusion, the concept of the divine heart of goodness is a profound and transformative belief that guides us towards embodying the highest expressions of love, compassion, and wisdom. It reminds us of our inherent divinity and our interconnectedness with all beings. By embracing our divine nature, we become catalysts for positive change, contributing to a more harmonious, compassionate, and sustainable world. May we all awaken to the divine heart of goodness within us and radiate its light to uplift and transform the world. Certainly! Here are extended explanations and reflections on the quotes from Jesus about the heart:

1. "Blessed are the pure in heart, for they will see God." - Matthew 5:8

In this profound statement, Jesus teaches that those who have pure hearts are truly blessed. A pure heart is one that is free from impurity, deceit, and wickedness. It is a heart that is sincere, genuine, and filled with love and goodness. When our hearts are pure, we are able to see and experience the presence of God in our lives. It is through the lens of purity that we can recognize the divine in ourselves and in others. This quote encourages us to cultivate purity in our hearts by striving for integrity, honesty, and righteousness. It calls us to seek sincerity in our thoughts and actions, to live with authenticity and transparency, and to align our hearts with God's will. When our hearts are pure, our vision becomes clear, and we are able to perceive the beauty, truth, and goodness that God has placed in the world.

1. "Love the Lord your God with all your heart and with all your soul and with all your mind." - Matthew 22:37

In this commandment, Jesus emphasizes the paramount importance of wholehearted love and devotion to God. It is a call to offer our complete selves to Him, holding nothing back. Loving God with all our heart, soul, and mind means engaging every aspect of our being in a deep and meaningful relationship with Him. It involves our emotions, our spirituality, and our intellect. Loving God with our heart means engaging our emotions and affections, allowing our love for Him to be genuine and passionate. Loving God with our soul involves deepening our spiritual connection with Him, recognizing that our souls find their ultimate fulfillment in communion with Him. Loving God with our mind calls us to engage our intellect, seeking to understand His teachings and applying them to our lives. This commandment challenges us to examine our hearts and ensure that our love for God is genuine, fervent, and all-encompassing. It calls us to prioritize our relationship with God above all else and to seek an intimate and profound connection with Him.

1. "For where your treasure is, there your heart will be also." - Matthew 6:21

Jesus's words highlight the profound connection between our hearts and our deepest desires. Our hearts naturally gravitate towards that which we value and consider as treasures. If our treasures are focused on material possessions, wealth, or worldly achievements, our hearts will be entangled in the pursuit of these things. However, if our treasures are rooted in spiritual values, love, compassion, and the Kingdom of God, our hearts will be focused on seeking and cultivating these qualities. This quote serves as a reminder to examine where our true treasures lie and to align our hearts with what truly matters in life. It calls us to prioritize eternal treasures over temporary ones and to seek fulfillment in spiritual growth and service to others. When our hearts are set on heavenly treasures, we are liberated from the bondage of materialism and find contentment and purpose in living out God's purposes.

1. "A good man brings good things out of the good stored up in his heart, and an evil man brings evil things out of the evil stored up in his heart. For the mouth speaks what the heart is full of." - Luke 6:45

Jesus's teaching emphasizes the intrinsic connection between the words we speak and the condition of our hearts. Our words are a reflection of what is stored in our hearts. If our hearts are filled with goodness, love, and righteousness, our words will reflect these qualities. On the other hand, if our hearts are filled with evil, hatred, or selfishness, our words will reveal these negative aspects. This quote reminds us of the importance of guarding our hearts, cultivating positive qualities within ourselves, and being mindful of the impact our words can have on others. It urges us to pay attention to the condition of our hearts, as it is from the overflow of our hearts that our words and actions flow. By nurturing a heart that is filled with love, compassion, and goodness, we can bring forth positive and life-giving words that bless and inspire those around us.

These quotes from Jesus provide profound insights into the nature of the heart and its significance in our spiritual journey. They invite us to reflect on the state of our hearts and to strive for purity, love, and righteousness. They remind us that our hearts play a central role in our relationship with God, in our interactions with others, and in the choices we make. Embracing the teachings of Jesus and nurturing a heart aligned with love and goodness allows us to experience the transformative power of God's presence in our lives and to radiate His light to the world around us. May we strive to have pure hearts, love God wholeheartedly, treasure heavenly things, and let our words be a reflection of the goodness stored in our hearts. Let us continually seek to cultivate our hearts, allowing them to be vessels of love, compassion, and righteousness, and to be transformed by the power of God's grace.

Living a good life

Living a good life is a profound and multifaceted pursuit that encompasses a wide range of dimensions and considerations. It involves finding harmony, fulfillment, and purpose in various aspects of our existence, including relationships, personal growth, contribution to society, self-care, and connection with something greater than ourselves.

One crucial aspect of living a good life is cultivating and nurturing healthy and fulfilling relationships. Meaningful connections with family, friends, romantic partners, and the community provide us with a sense of belonging, support, and love. Building and maintaining strong relationships involve qualities such as effective communication, empathy, trust, and mutual respect. By investing time and effort into fostering these connections, we create a network of support, love, and understanding that enriches our lives and enhances our overall well-being.

Living a good life also involves continuous personal growth and self-improvement. This can manifest in various ways, such as setting and pursuing meaningful goals, honing our skills and talents, and embracing opportunities for learning and development. Engaging in self-reflection, seeking new experiences, and stepping outside our comfort zones can lead to personal transformation, expanded perspectives, and a deeper understanding of ourselves and the world around us. By committing to our personal growth, we unlock our potential and open ourselves up to new possibilities and opportunities for fulfillment.

Contributing to the well-being of others and making a positive impact in our communities and society is another vital aspect of living a good life. Acts of kindness, generosity, and service not only benefit those in need but also bring a sense of purpose, fulfillment, and connection. By using our skills, resources, and influence to address social issues, promote justice, and create positive change, we contribute to a more compassionate, equitable, and thriving world. Engaging in volunteer work, supporting charitable causes, or advocating for social justice are all ways in which we can make a difference and leave a lasting impact.

Moreover, self-care is an essential component of living a good life. Taking care of our physical, mental, and emotional well-being allows us to show up fully in our lives and pursue our goals and aspirations. This can involve practices such as regular exercise, healthy eating, getting enough rest, and engaging in activities that bring us joy, relaxation, and rejuvenation. Prioritizing self-care helps us maintain balance, resilience, and overall well-being, enabling us to navigate life's challenges with grace and strength.

Living a good life also encompasses finding meaning and purpose. This involves exploring our values, passions, and interests and aligning our actions with what brings us a sense of fulfillment and satisfaction. Whether through meaningful work, creative pursuits, spiritual practices, or a commitment to a cause, finding purpose allows us to live with intention, authenticity, and a deep sense of meaning. It gives us a sense of direction and a reason to wake up each day with enthusiasm and gratitude.

Additionally, connecting with something greater than ourselves can contribute to a sense of transcendence and purpose in life. This can take the form of spirituality, religious beliefs, or a connection with nature, the universe, or humanity as a whole. Cultivating a sense of awe, wonder, and gratitude for the beauty and interconnectedness of all things can deepen our sense of meaning and provide guidance and solace during challenging times. It allows us to tap into a source of wisdom, strength, and inspiration that transcends our individual selves.

Living a good life also involves embracing resilience and navigating adversity with grace and strength. Life is filled with ups and downs, and our ability to bounce back, learn from setbacks, and adapt to change plays a significant role in our overall well-being and happiness. Developing resilience allows us to face challenges with optimism, perseverance, and a growth mindset, enabling us to overcome obstacles and continue moving forward on our path to a good life. It teaches us valuable lessons, enhances our self-belief, and strengthens our inner resolve.

In conclusion, living a good life is a lifelong and deeply personal journey of self-discovery, growth, and contribution. It involves cultivating healthy and fulfilling relationships, pursuing personal growth, contributing to the well-being of others, practicing self-care, finding meaning and purpose, connecting with something greater than ourselves, and embracing resilience. By integrating these elements into our lives, we can create a life that is meaningful, fulfilling, and aligned with our deepest values and aspirations. It is a continuous process of learning, evolving, and striving to become the best version of ourselves while making a positive impact on the world around us.

Destruction of the Heart

Self-destruction is a deeply complex and multifaceted phenomenon that encompasses a wide range of interconnected factors. It refers to the intentional act of causing harm or damage to oneself, whether it be physical, emotional, or mental. Understanding the intricacies of self-destruction is crucial in order to provide comprehensive support and intervention for individuals who are struggling.

At its core, self-destruction often emerges from deep-seated emotional pain, trauma, or distress. It can be a response to overwhelming feelings of sadness, anger, guilt, or shame that an individual may struggle to cope with. These intense emotions, if left unaddressed, can create a strong internal turmoil that drives individuals towards self-destructive behaviors as a means of escape or relief.

Self-destruction can manifest in various ways, depending on the individual and their unique circumstances. Some common examples include self-harm, substance abuse, disordered eating, compulsive behaviors, or engaging in risky activities. These behaviors serve as temporary coping mechanisms, providing a sense of control or distraction from emotional pain. However, they ultimately perpetuate the cycle of self-destruction, leading to further harm and difficulties.

Underlying self-destructive behaviors are often negative thought patterns and distorted beliefs about oneself. Individuals who engage in self-destruction may experience feelings of worthlessness, self-blame, or a pervasive sense of being irreparably damaged. These negative beliefs can contribute to a vicious cycle where self-destructive behaviors reinforce negative self-perceptions, further fueling the desire to engage in harmful actions.

External factors, such as societal pressures, trauma, or a lack of healthy support systems, can also play a role in self-destruction. In a culture that often emphasizes achievement, beauty, and material success, individuals may feel immense pressure to meet societal expectations, leading to feelings of inadequacy or a sense of failure. Additionally, experiences of trauma, abuse, or neglect can significantly impact an individual's mental and emotional well-being, increasing the risk of self-destructive behaviors.

Addressing self-destruction requires a multifaceted approach that considers the individual's unique circumstances and needs. It involves providing individuals with the tools and support to develop healthier coping mechanisms, build resilience, and challenge negative thought patterns. Therapy, counseling, or support groups can be invaluable in helping individuals explore the root causes of their self-destructive behaviors, navigate through their emotions, and develop strategies for healing and growth.

Creating a supportive and compassionate environment is also essential in combating self-destruction. Breaking the stigma surrounding mental health, fostering open conversations, and promoting understanding and empathy can encourage individuals to seek help and reduce feelings of isolation. Building strong social connections, fostering a sense of belonging, and providing access to community resources can help individuals find healthier ways to cope with their pain and develop a support system that understands and validates their struggles.

Recovery from self-destruction is a deeply personal and ongoing journey. It requires commitment, self-reflection, and a willingness to confront and heal from past traumas or wounds. It involves learning new coping strategies, developing self-compassion and self-worth, and cultivating a sense of purpose and meaning in life.

It is important to recognize that overcoming self-destruction is not a linear process, and setbacks may occur along the way. However, with consistent effort, professional support, and a strong support system, individuals can break free from the destructive patterns, heal their wounds, and embark on a path of self-discovery, growth, and personal transformation.

If you or someone you know is struggling with self-destructive behaviors, it is crucial to seek help from mental health professionals or helplines. Remember, recovery is possible, and there is hope for a brighter future. Together, we can work towards breaking the cycle of self-destruction and fostering a society that prioritizes empathy, understanding, and support for those who are hurting.

In conclusion, self-destruction is a deeply complex and multifaceted phenomenon that involves intentional harm towards oneself. It is driven by deep emotional pain, negative thought patterns, societal pressures, and a lack of healthy support systems. Addressing self-destruction requires a comprehensive approach that includes therapy, support groups, and creating a compassionate environment. Recovery is an ongoing journey that involves developing healthier coping mechanisms, building resilience, and cultivating self-compassion. By fostering understanding, empathy, and support, we can help individuals break free from self-destruction and create a brighter future for themselves.

The Heart of Humans

"The Heart of Humans" is an extraordinary and awe-inspiring aspect of our existence that encompasses the very essence of our humanity. It is a vast and boundless landscape that pulsates with the rhythm of emotions, the depth of values, and the power of profound connections. The heart of humans is a tapestry of complexity and intricacy, intricately woven with the threads of our experiences, guiding our choices, and illuminating our purpose in life.

At its core, the heart of humans is a wellspring of boundless love, compassion, and empathy. It is through our hearts that we forge genuine and deep connections with others, fostering a sense of belonging, understanding, and unity. Our hearts enable us to extend kindness, empathy, and care to those around us, creating a ripple effect of compassion that reverberates throughout the world. The heart of humans is a beacon of light in times of darkness, a source of comfort and solace for those in need, and a catalyst for positive change in our communities.

Moreover, the heart of humans is a sanctuary of emotions, a canvas upon which the full spectrum of human feelings is painted. It is within our hearts that we experience the sublime heights of joy, love, and happiness, as well as the depths of sorrow, grief, and pain. Our hearts are the conduits through which emotions flow, guiding our responses to the world and shaping our perceptions of reality. Through our hearts, we navigate the intricacies of our inner landscape, cultivating self-awareness, and deepening our understanding of ourselves and others.

Furthermore, the heart of humans is the sacred abode of our values and beliefs. It is within our hearts that we hold our most cherished convictions, shaping our moral compass, and influencing the choices we make. Our hearts resonate with principles of integrity, justice, and compassion, guiding us towards a life of purpose, meaning, and significance. The heart of humans serves as a guiding light, illuminating the path towards righteousness and inspiring us to make a positive impact on the world around us.

In addition, the heart of humans is a profound source of identity and self-expression. It is within our hearts that our truest selves reside, embracing the uniqueness, passions, and desires that define us. Our hearts hold the key to our dreams, aspirations, and hopes, fueling our pursuit of personal growth, self-fulfillment, and self-actualization. Through our hearts, we find the courage to embrace our authentic selves, to express our passions boldly, and to live in alignment with our deepest values and aspirations. The heart of humans empowers us to shine our light brightly, leaving an indelible mark on the tapestry of human existence.

Moreover, the heart of humans is an infinite reservoir of resilience and strength. It is through our hearts that we find the inner fortitude to face adversity, overcome challenges, and persevere in the face of obstacles. Our hearts provide us with the courage to step outside our comfort zones, to learn from our failures, and to grow from our experiences. It is through our hearts that we develop the strength to navigate the ebb and flow of life, emerging stronger, wiser, and more resilient. The heart of humans sustains us in times of darkness, fuels our determination, and empowers us to embrace the fullness of life's journey.

In essence, the heart of humans is an intricate and magnificent symphony, an embodiment of the beauty, complexity, and resilience of our shared humanity. It is the core of our being, connecting us to ourselves, to others, and to the world at large. Embracing and nurturing the heart of humans allows us to live a life characterized by authenticity, kindness, and purpose. It is through the depths of our hearts that we create a more compassionate, understanding, and harmonious world for all. The heart of humans is a testament to the limitless potential and profound impact we have as individuals and as a collective, illuminating the path to a brighter and more compassionate future for generations to come.

The core of the heart refers to its central and essential part. In the context of the text provided, "The Heart of Humans," the phrase "core of the heart" is used metaphorically to represent the central themes, messages, or essence of the human being. It signifies the fundamental aspects of self-discovery, the power of belief in hope and faith.

Hope

Hope is a profound and complex emotion that transcends the boundaries of time and circumstance. It is a fundamental aspect of the human experience, deeply ingrained in our hearts and minds. Hope is a beacon of light that shines through the darkness, illuminating our path and fueling our dreams.

At its core, hope is a powerful force that nourishes our spirit and sustains us during challenging times. It is the belief in the possibility of a better future, even when faced with uncertainty and adversity. Hope allows us to envision a world where dreams can be realized, where obstacles can be overcome, and where joy, peace, and fulfillment abound.

Hope is not a passive state of mind; it is an active choice. It requires courage, perseverance, and resilience. Hope empowers us to rise above our circumstances, to forge ahead despite setbacks, and to create positive change in our lives and in the world around us. It is a catalyst for growth, transformation, and personal development.

Hope is deeply intertwined with faith and trust. It requires us to have faith in ourselves, in others, and in the divine. It is the unwavering belief that there is a higher purpose guiding our journey, that there is meaning in our experiences, and that there are forces at work beyond what we can see. Hope invites us to surrender control and to trust in the unfolding of life, knowing that even in the midst of challenges, something greater is at play.

Hope is contagious and has the power to inspire and uplift others. When we embody hope, we become beacons of positivity and encouragement, radiating optimism and resilience to those around us. Our hope can inspire others to believe in themselves, to overcome their own obstacles, and to strive for a better future. Through our actions and words, we can create a ripple effect of hope, spreading its transformative power far and wide.

Hope is not limited to individual pursuits; it extends to collective aspirations as well. It is the driving force behind social movements, advocacy, and the pursuit of justice and equality. Hope fuels our determination to create a more compassionate, inclusive, and sustainable world. It propels us to take action, to challenge the status quo, and to work towards a future where everyone can thrive.

In times of darkness and despair, hope provides solace and comfort. It is the light that guides us through the storm, reminding us that there is always a glimmer of hope, no matter how small. Hope allows us to find strength in the face of adversity, to hold onto resilience when faced with challenges, and to emerge stronger and wiser on the other side.

Hope is not immune to the realities of life. It acknowledges the presence of pain, suffering, and loss. However, it refuses to be defined by them. Hope allows us to find beauty and meaning in the midst of hardship, to learn and grow from our experiences, and to find purpose in our journey.

In conclusion, hope is a powerful and transformative force that resides within the human spirit. It is the belief in the potential for a better future, the courage to rise above challenges, and the resilience to keep moving forward. Hope is a guiding light that leads us towards our dreams and aspirations, nourishing our souls and inspiring us to create a world filled with love, compassion, and possibility.

Darkness and Despair

In the vast tapestry of human existence, darkness and despair are inevitable threads that weave their way into the fabric of our lives. They represent the moments when we find ourselves enveloped in a cloud of heaviness, where the weight of our struggles and pain seems insurmountable. It is during these times that we may feel a sense of hopelessness, as if there is no escape from the abyss of despair.

Darkness, in its various forms, can manifest as emotional turmoil, mental anguish, or a sense of emptiness. It may be brought on by external circumstances such as loss, betrayal, or failure, or it may emerge from within, stemming from deep-rooted insecurities or unresolved traumas. Regardless of its origins, darkness has the power to cast a shadow over every aspect of our lives, leaving us feeling disconnected, isolated, and trapped.

In the depths of darkness, our thoughts may become distorted, and our perspective may become clouded. We may lose sight of our own worth, our potential, and the possibilities that lie ahead. The darkness may whisper lies of unworthiness, hopelessness, and a bleak future. It can feel like an inescapable prison, confining us to a life devoid of joy, purpose, and fulfillment.

Despair, on the other hand, is the emotional response to the darkness that engulfs us. It is a profound sadness, a feeling of utter hopelessness and resignation. It drains us of our energy, dampens our spirits, and obscures our vision of a brighter future. Despair can make us question our worth, our purpose, and our ability to overcome the challenges that life throws our way.

Yet, even in the depths of darkness and despair, there is a glimmer of light that beckons us forward. It is the flicker of hope, the belief that there is a way out of the darkness and into a life filled with meaning, joy, and fulfillment. Hope is the antidote to despair, the guiding star that leads us out of the labyrinth of darkness and towards a brighter tomorrow.

Hope is the belief that there is a purpose to our pain, that our struggles have meaning, and that there is a greater plan at work. It is the unwavering faith that there is light at the end of the tunnel, even when all seems lost. Hope fuels our resilience, our determination to keep moving forward despite the challenges we face. It reminds us that we are not alone in our struggles, that there are others who have walked similar paths and emerged stronger on the other side.

Finding hope in the midst of darkness and despair is not always easy. It requires a shift in perspective, a conscious choice to focus on the possibilities rather than the limitations. It may involve seeking support from loved ones, therapists, or support groups who can provide guidance, encouragement, and a listening ear. It may also entail engaging in self-care practices that nourish our minds, bodies, and spirits, such as meditation, exercise, or creative expression.

Ultimately, the journey from darkness and despair to light and hope is a deeply personal one. It is a process of self-discovery, healing, and growth. It may involve facing our fears, confronting our past traumas, and making difficult choices. It requires patience, perseverance, and a willingness to embrace vulnerability.

But as we navigate through the darkness, inching closer to the light, we begin to realize that our struggles have not defined us, but have shaped us into stronger, more compassionate, and resilient individuals. We discover that within us lies a wellspring of strength and courage, waiting to be tapped into. And we come to understand that darkness and despair, though painful and challenging, can be catalysts for growth, transformation, and a deeper appreciation for the light that shines within us and around us.

So, if you find yourself in the midst of darkness and despair, know that you are not alone. Reach out for help, hold onto hope, and trust in your own inner resilience. Remember that the dawn always follows the darkest night, and that within you lies the power to create a life filled with purpose, joy, and fulfillment. Embrace the journey, for it is through the darkness that we truly learn to appreciate the light.

In the face of darkness and despair, it is important to remember that seeking support is a sign of strength, not weakness. Whether it be the support of loved ones, therapists, or support groups, reaching out to others can provide a lifeline of hope and understanding. Sharing our struggles and fears can help to alleviate the burden we carry and remind us that we are not alone in our journey.

Additionally, embracing self-care practices can be a powerful tool in navigating through darkness. Engaging in activities that bring joy, relaxation, and rejuvenation can help to lift our spirits and provide a respite from the weight of despair. Taking care of our physical, mental, and emotional well-being is crucial during these challenging times.

Moreover, cultivating a mindset of gratitude and focusing on the positive aspects of our lives can help to counteract the darkness that surrounds us. Even in the midst of despair, there are often moments of beauty, love, and connection that we can hold onto. By shifting our focus towards these moments, we can find strength and hope in the midst of adversity.

Ultimately, it is important to remember that darkness and despair are not permanent states, but temporary experiences that are a part of the human condition. Just as the night gives way to the dawn, so too do our struggles give way to growth and transformation. By embracing hope, seeking support, and practicing self-care, we can navigate through the darkness and emerge stronger, wiser, and more resilient.

In conclusion, darkness and despair are inevitable parts of the human experience. They can leave us feeling lost, isolated, and drained of hope. However, within these moments of darkness, there is always a glimmer of light that beckons us forward. Hope, resilience, and the support of others can help guide us through the darkness and into a life filled with purpose, joy, and fulfillment. Remember that you are not alone in your struggles and that the journey towards healing and growth is possible. Embrace the journey, for it is through the darkness that we learn to appreciate the light.

No Escaping The "Heart"

The question of whether we can escape our hearts invites us to embark on a profound exploration of the human experience and the intricate interplay between our emotions, desires, and the very essence of our being. It beckons us to delve deeper into the depths of our hearts and unravel the complex tapestry of our innermost selves.

Our hearts, metaphorically representing the core of our existence, serve as the epicenter of our emotions, the reservoir of our desires, and the seat of our humanity. They are the conduit through which our emotions flow, infusing our lives with a kaleidoscope of experiences. From the heights of love and joy to the depths of sorrow and pain, our emotions give texture and meaning to our journey, shaping our perceptions, guiding our choices, and forming the foundation of our relationships.

Moreover, our hearts house our deepest desires, the yearnings and longings that drive us forward on our path of self-discovery and personal growth. These desires embody the essence of our aspirations, dreams, and passions. They act as the propelling force behind our actions, urging us to transcend limitations, overcome obstacles, and strive for the highest expression of ourselves.

Attempting to escape or ignore our hearts, our emotions, and our desires can have profound consequences on our well-being and overall sense of fulfillment. When we suppress or deny our emotions, they can fester within us, manifesting in physical ailments, mental distress, and a deep sense of disconnection. Similarly, neglecting our desires can leave us feeling unfulfilled, adrift, and disconnected from our true purpose.

Embracing and understanding our hearts, however, opens the gateway to a life lived authentically and wholeheartedly. It involves acknowledging and accepting the full range of our emotions, embracing the complexity and depth of our inner world with compassion and self-awareness. By embracing our emotions, we cultivate emotional intelligence, deepen our understanding of ourselves and others, and develop the resilience to navigate life's challenges with grace and wisdom.

Likewise, honoring and exploring our desires empowers us to live lives in alignment with our true selves. It entails listening to the whispers of our hearts, discerning the yearnings that stir within us, and embracing the path that resonates with our deepest values and aspirations. Embracing our desires infuses our lives with purpose, passion, and a profound sense of meaning and fulfillment.

It is crucial to recognize that embracing our hearts does not mean being enslaved by our emotions or desires. Rather, it involves cultivating a healthy relationship with them, harnessing their power, and channeling their energy in constructive and transformative ways. By understanding the messages behind our emotions and desires, we gain insight into our innermost needs, longings, and aspirations, enabling us to make conscious choices, set meaningful goals, and live with authenticity and intention.

In essence, the question of whether we can escape our hearts invites us to embark on a profound journey of self-discovery and self-acceptance. Our hearts are an integral part of our existence, intricately woven into the fabric of who we are. Instead of attempting to evade or suppress them, it is essential to honor and embrace our hearts, our emotions, and our desires. Through this embrace, we unlock the door to a life filled with depth, meaning, and connection—a life where we can fully express our humanity, forge deep and meaningful relationships, and create a world that celebrates the beauty and complexity of the human heart.

Memories and Desires

Memory and desire are intricate and interwoven components of the thought process in humans, exerting profound influence over our thoughts, motivations, and decision-making. These cognitive processes are essential for our ability to navigate the world, form meaningful connections, and pursue our goals and aspirations.

Memory, at its core, refers to our capacity to encode, store, and retrieve information and past experiences. It is a multifaceted process that involves various stages and systems within the brain. Encoding allows us to transform sensory input into meaningful representations that can be stored. Storage involves the consolidation and organization of information into different memory systems, such as sensory memory, short-term memory, and long-term memory. Retrieval is the process of accessing and bringing forth stored information when needed.

Sensory memory serves as a temporary holding place for sensory information, allowing us to perceive the world as a continuous stream of events. Short-term memory, also known as working memory, enables us to temporarily hold and manipulate information for immediate use. However, its capacity is limited, and information is easily forgotten unless it is rehearsed or transferred to long-term memory. Long-term memory has an extensive capacity and stores information over an extended period. It is further divided into explicit memory, which involves conscious recall of facts and events, and implicit memory, which influences behavior without conscious awareness.

Memory retrieval is the process of accessing stored information from long-term memory. Retrieval cues, such as associations, contextual details, or emotional triggers, help activate the relevant memory traces. The retrieval process can be influenced by factors like the strength of the memory trace, the emotional significance of the information, and the context in which the memory was initially encoded. Memories can be consciously retrieved through intentional recall or unconsciously accessed through priming effects or recognition.

Desire, on the other hand, encompasses our wants, needs, and motivations. It is the driving force behind our thoughts, actions, and decision-making. Desires can originate from various sources, including biological, psychological, and social factors. Biological desires arise from our basic survival needs, such as hunger, thirst, and sexual reproduction. Psychological desires encompass higher-level needs, such as the need for love, belonging, achievement, and self-actualization. Social desires are influenced by cultural norms, societal expectations, and personal values.

Desires can be conscious or unconscious, and they range from simple to complex. They shape our goals, aspirations, and preferences, serving as powerful motivators for our behavior. Desires influence the allocation of our attention, guide our decision-making processes, and determine the actions we take to fulfill our needs and wants. They shape our perceptions of what is valuable, meaningful, and fulfilling in our lives.

In the thought process, memory and desire dynamically interact and mutually influence each other. Our memories, stored in long-term memory, influence our desires by shaping our preferences, expectations, and emotional responses. Positive memories associated with past experiences can create a desire to recreate those experiences, while negative memories can generate aversions and a desire to avoid similar situations. Memories also contribute to the formation of desires by providing us with a reference point for what we find pleasurable, rewarding, or challenging.

Conversely, desires can influence our memory processes by directing our attention and focus. When we have a strong desire for something, it can enhance our memory encoding and retrieval processes. Motivation and emotional significance can facilitate the consolidation of memories, making them more likely to be retained and retrieved. For instance, when we are highly motivated to learn a new skill or achieve a goal, we are more likely to pay attention, practice, and remember relevant information.

Moreover, the thought process involves the interplay between memory and desire in decision-making. Our memories provide us with a vast reservoir of information and past experiences that we can draw upon to evaluate options, make predictions, and make informed choices. Our desires, however, guide our preferences, priorities, and subjective evaluations of different options. They influence the weighting and evaluation of potential outcomes, helping us select the course of action that aligns with our goals and desires.

The interaction between memory and desire in decision-making is complex and influenced by various cognitive, emotional, and social factors. Our memories inform our desires by shaping our expectations, beliefs, and preferences. In turn, our desires influence our memory by directing our attention, encoding processes, and retrieval strategies toward information relevant to our goals and motivations.

In summary, memory and desire are intricately linked in the thought process of humans. Memory enables us to encode, store, and retrieve information and past experiences, providing us with a cognitive framework for understanding the world and making decisions. Desire, on the other hand, shapes our wants, needs, and motivations, driving our thoughts, actions, and choices. The interplay between memory and desire is dynamic and multifaceted, influencing our preferences, goals, and decision-making processes as we navigate the complexities of human cognition. Understanding the profound relationship between memory and desire offers valuable insights into the workings of the human mind and the factors that drive our thoughts, motivations, and behaviors.

Moral Capacity

"Moral capacity," a fundamental aspect of human nature, encompasses a vast and intricate array of interconnected cognitive, emotional, and behavioral dimensions related to ethics and morality. It represents the innate potential within individuals to understand, evaluate, and act upon moral principles, shaping their behavior, decision-making, and relationships with others in profound ways.

Cognitive aspects of moral capacity involve the acquisition, assimilation, and application of moral knowledge and reasoning. This includes developing a deep understanding of ethical theories, principles, and values that form the foundation for moral judgment. It involves the ability to critically analyze complex moral dilemmas, consider multiple perspectives, and weigh the potential consequences of actions in light of ethical standards.

Emotional aspects of moral capacity encompass the affective responses and motivations that underpin moral behavior. Empathy, a cornerstone of moral capacity, allows individuals to connect with others on a deep emotional level, fostering compassion, care, and a genuine concern for the well-being of others. Moral emotions, such as guilt, shame, and moral indignation, also play a vital role in moral capacity by shaping individuals' moral judgments and motivating them to act in alignment with their moral values.

Behavioral aspects of moral capacity involve the translation of moral knowledge and emotional responses into ethical action. It encompasses the ability to consistently act in accordance with moral principles, even in challenging or conflicting situations. This requires moral courage, the willingness to stand up for one's ethical beliefs and values, and the demonstration of moral integrity by consistently embodying ethical behavior in one's actions and choices.

Furthermore, moral capacity is deeply influenced by social and cultural factors. Society, through its norms, values, and ethical frameworks, shapes individuals' understanding of what is considered right and wrong. Cultural diversity enriches moral capacity by exposing individuals to a variety of moral perspectives, challenging biases, and fostering a more inclusive and nuanced understanding of morality.

Moral capacity is not a fixed trait but can be nurtured, developed, and refined throughout one's lifetime. Moral education and reflection play pivotal roles in fostering the growth of moral capacity. By providing individuals with opportunities to engage in ethical discussions, explore their values, and critically examine their own moral reasoning, moral education cultivates moral reasoning skills and fosters the development of moral character.

Ultimately, moral capacity is indispensable for individuals to navigate the complexities of life and make ethical decisions that promote the well-being of themselves and others. It enables individuals to consider the broader implications of their actions, make choices that align with their values, and contribute to the creation of a more just, compassionate, and harmonious society.

In conclusion, moral capacity encompasses a rich tapestry of interconnected cognitive, emotional, and behavioral dimensions related to ethics and morality. It involves the acquisition of moral knowledge, the cultivation of moral reasoning and emotional responses, and the embodiment of ethical action. Nurturing and expanding moral capacity is not only essential but also transformative, empowering individuals to make informed and responsible moral choices that contribute to the betterment of themselves and the world they inhabit.

Life

Life is a profound and enigmatic phenomenon that encompasses the essence of existence itself. It is the intricate interplay of countless elements, from the microscopic building blocks of cells to the grand tapestry of ecosystems that span the globe. Life is a symphony of complexity, diversity, and interconnectedness that unfolds on a breathtaking scale.

At its core, life is defined by the presence of living organisms. These organisms possess the remarkable ability to grow, reproduce, metabolize, and respond to their environment. From the smallest single-celled organisms to the majestic complexity of human beings, life manifests in an astonishing variety of forms, each with its own unique characteristics and adaptations.

Life is a journey, a continuous process of growth, development, and transformation. It is a dance between stability and change, as organisms strive to maintain equilibrium in the face of ever-shifting circumstances. From the delicate balance of ecosystems to the intricate workings of cells within our bodies, life is a constant negotiation between preservation and adaptation.

Life is not confined to individual organisms but extends to the dynamic interactions between them. It is the web of relationships that weaves together every living being on Earth. From the complex social structures of ants to the intricate symbiotic partnerships between plants and pollinators, life is a tapestry of interdependence and collaboration.

Beyond the physical manifestations, life encompasses the intangible aspects of consciousness, cognition, and emotion. It is the spark of awareness that illuminates the human experience, fueling our thoughts, desires, and aspirations. Life is the canvas upon which we paint our stories, with each individual weaving a unique narrative through their relationships, achievements, and contributions.

The meaning and purpose of life are deeply personal and subjective, shaped by individual perspectives, beliefs, and values. For some, life is a quest for knowledge and understanding, a relentless pursuit of truth and enlightenment. For others, life is a celebration of joy, love, and connection, finding fulfillment in the richness of human relationships. And for some, life is a journey of self-discovery and personal growth, a constant striving to become the best version of oneself.

Life is a precious gift, a fleeting and fragile existence that calls upon us to cherish every moment. It is an invitation to embrace the beauty, wonder, and mystery of the world around us. Life is an opportunity to make a difference, to leave a positive impact on the lives of others and the planet we call home.

In the grand tapestry of existence, life is a thread that weaves together the past, present, and future. It is a reminder of our shared humanity, connecting us to the countless generations that have come before and those that will follow. Life is a testament to resilience, adaptability, and the capacity for growth and transformation.

Ultimately, life is a journey of discovery and meaning, an exploration of the vast potential that resides within each of us. It is an invitation to embrace the fullness of our existence, to cultivate compassion, curiosity, and gratitude. Life is a precious and fleeting gift, and it is up to us to make the most of it, to live with purpose, passion, and a deep appreciation for the miracle of being alive.

Purpose

The purpose of humans is a profound and multifaceted topic that has captivated the minds and hearts of individuals across cultures and civilizations throughout history. It is a question that invites us to explore the depths of our existence, the intricacies of our consciousness, and the interconnectedness of all life.

The concept of human purpose encompasses a wide range of perspectives, beliefs, and philosophies. From a religious standpoint, many faith traditions propose that humans have a purpose rooted in their relationship with a higher power or divine plan. For example, in Christianity, the purpose of humans is often seen as glorifying God, living in accordance with moral principles, and striving for spiritual growth and salvation. Similarly, in Buddhism, the purpose of humans is to attain enlightenment and break free from the cycle of suffering through the practice of compassion, wisdom, and mindfulness.

From a secular standpoint, the purpose of humans can be seen as a journey of self-discovery and personal growth. It involves exploring one's passions, values, and talents, and aligning one's actions and choices with these inner truths. The pursuit of happiness, fulfillment, and meaningful connections with others is often at the core of secular understandings of human purpose. This perspective emphasizes the importance of self-actualization, personal development, and making a positive impact on the world.

In addition to individual purposes, humans also have a collective purpose as members of society. This includes contributing to the well-being of others, fostering social harmony, and working towards the greater good. Many people find purpose in roles such as being a parent, a teacher, a healthcare professional, or an advocate for social justice. By engaging in acts of kindness, compassion, and service, individuals can find a deeper sense of purpose and connection to their communities.

Furthermore, the purpose of humans can be seen from an evolutionary perspective. As a species, humans have evolved with certain capacities and abilities that have allowed them to thrive and adapt to their environments. From this viewpoint, the purpose of humans can be seen as contributing to the survival and flourishing of the human species. This includes aspects such as reproduction, caring for offspring, and maintaining social connections and cooperation.

Moreover, the purpose of humans can be seen in the context of the broader natural world. Humans are part of a vast ecosystem, interconnected with other species and the environment. The purpose of humans, then, can be understood as being responsible stewards of the Earth, taking care of the planet and its resources for present and future generations. This perspective emphasizes the importance of sustainable living, environmental conservation, and promoting ecological balance.

Additionally, the purpose of humans can be found in the pursuit of knowledge, discovery, and the advancement of civilization. Throughout history, humans have demonstrated a remarkable curiosity and drive to understand the world and push the boundaries of what is possible. From scientific exploration to artistic expression, humans have a deep-seated desire to expand their understanding, creativity, and innovation. The purpose of humans in this context is to contribute to the collective knowledge and progress of humanity.

Moreover, the purpose of humans can be seen in the context of love and connection. Humans are social beings, wired for relationships and community. The purpose of humans, then, can be understood as cultivating deep connections, empathy, and compassion. By nurturing relationships, practicing kindness, and fostering understanding, humans can create a more harmonious and interconnected world.

Furthermore, the purpose of humans can be seen in the pursuit of justice and equality. Throughout history, humans have fought for and continue to fight for the rights and dignity of all individuals. The purpose of humans in this context is to challenge systems of inequality, advocate for justice, and create a more equitable society. This includes addressing issues such as poverty, discrimination, and oppression.

Ultimately, the purpose of humans is a deeply personal and profound quest. It is a journey that invites.

The Core

Deep within the intricate chambers of the human heart lies a profound and expansive core that encapsulates the very essence of our existence. The core of the heart is a sacred space, a sanctuary where the myriad facets of our consciousness converge, intertwine, and create a tapestry of meaning, purpose, and connection.

At the core of the heart, we encounter the radiant flame of love, an eternal fire that burns within us. It is this love that fuels our relationships, binds us together in profound and meaningful ways, and gives our lives immeasurable depth and richness. The core of the heart resonates with the vibrations of compassion, empathy, and understanding, fostering a deep sense of interconnectedness with all living beings. It is through the core of the heart that we experience the profound joy of giving and receiving love, of nurturing and being nurtured, and of forging lasting connections that transcend time and space.

Moreover, the core of the heart is a boundless wellspring of personal growth and self-discovery. It is within this expansive space that we embark on a lifelong journey of exploration, continuously uncovering hidden depths within ourselves. The core of the heart serves as a compass, guiding us towards our true passions, purposes, and potentials. It is through the core of the heart that we tap into our unique gifts and talents, embracing our authentic selves and blossoming into the fullest expression of who we are.

At the core of the heart, we encounter the guiding light of our values and beliefs, the moral compass that directs our actions and shapes our character. It is within this space that we define our principles of integrity, justice, and kindness, and strive to live in alignment with them. The core of the heart inspires us to make choices that reflect our deepest-held convictions, to stand up for what is right, and to advocate for the well-being of all. It is through the core of the heart that we find the strength and resilience to navigate life's challenges with grace and integrity.

Furthermore, the core of the heart is an infinite reservoir of resilience and inner strength. It is within this space that we summon the courage to face adversity, to persevere in the face of obstacles, and to emerge stronger and more resilient than before. The core of the heart nurtures our ability to adapt, to learn from setbacks, and to transform challenges into opportunities for growth. It is through the core of the heart that we cultivate a steadfast belief in our own capacity to overcome, to rise above, and to thrive in the face of life's trials.

The core of the heart resonates with the harmonious melodies of purpose and meaning. It is within this space that we discover our unique calling, our contribution to the world, and our profound reason for being. The core of the heart ignites the fire of passion within us, propelling us towards our dreams, inspiring us to make a positive impact, and empowering us to leave a lasting legacy. It is through the core of the heart that we align our actions with our deepest desires, infusing our lives with purpose and significance.

At its core, the heart represents the epicenter of our humanity, the sacred sanctuary where love, growth, values, resilience, purpose, and connection converge. It is a space of profound introspection, self-understanding, and self-actualization. It is through the core of the heart that we come to realize the interconnectedness of all life, the vast tapestry of existence in which we are intricately woven. It is within this space that we recognize our collective responsibility to nurture compassion, promote justice, and create a world that embraces the inherent worth and dignity of every being.

In summary, the core of the heart is an expansive and sacred space within us that holds the essence of our humanity. It is a reservoir of love, compassion, personal growth, values, resilience, purpose, and connection. It is through the core of the heart that we embark on a transformative journey of self-discovery, forging deep connections with others, and leaving an indelible mark on the world. It is within this space that we discover the boundless depths of our own existence and the profound interconnectedness that unites us all.

Love

Love, the most powerful and mysterious of all human emotions, is a force that surpasses understanding and transcends the boundaries of time and space. It is a complex and multi-faceted phenomenon that has been the subject of countless poems, songs, and works of art throughout history. Love is both a profound feeling and an active choice, a deep affection that can encompass a wide range of emotions, experiences, and expressions.

At its core, love is a fundamental human need. It is an innate longing for connection, belonging, and intimacy that is deeply ingrained in our DNA. Love has the power to bring joy, fulfillment, and meaning to our lives, and it is often considered one of the driving forces behind human happiness and well-being.

Love can manifest in various forms, each with its own unique qualities and dynamics. Romantic love, often portrayed as a whirlwind of passion and desire, is a profound and intense emotional and physical attraction between two individuals. It is a love that can ignite sparks of excitement, infuse life with a newfound sense of purpose, and create a deep sense of intimacy and connection.

Familial love, the bond that exists between parents and children, siblings, or extended family members, is a love that is rooted in unconditional acceptance, support, and care. It is a love that knows no bounds, transcending differences and challenges, and providing a sense of security, belonging, and identity. Familial love is often characterized by a deep sense of loyalty, sacrifice, and commitment to the well-being and happiness of one another.

Friendship, a love that is built on trust, mutual respect, and shared experiences, is a unique and cherished bond that brings companionship, support, and a sense of belonging. Friends are the pillars of our lives, offering a safe space for vulnerability, laughter, and growth. Friendship love is a love that can withstand the test of time, distance, and life's ups and downs, providing unwavering support and understanding.

Love extends beyond personal relationships and encompasses a broader sense of connection with humanity as a whole. It is a love that recognizes the inherent worth and dignity of every individual, fostering empathy, compassion, and a commitment to social justice and equality. This love inspires acts of kindness, generosity, and advocacy for the well-being of others, creating a ripple effect that can transform communities and societies.

Love is not without its challenges. It can be accompanied by feelings of vulnerability, fear, and the potential for heartbreak. Love requires effort, communication, and a willingness to navigate the complexities that arise in relationships. It requires the courage to be open, vulnerable, and authentic, to prioritize the needs and happiness of others, and to embrace the imperfections and growth that come with love.

Yet, despite the challenges, love has the power to transform individuals and societies. It can inspire personal growth, promote social harmony, and foster a more compassionate and inclusive world. Love has the capacity to heal wounds, bridge divides, and create a sense of unity and understanding. It is through love that we can build meaningful connections, find purpose and fulfillment, and leave a lasting legacy of compassion and kindness.

Love is not confined to the realm of human relationships alone; it extends to our connection with the natural world. Love for nature, the environment, and all living beings fuels our desire to protect and preserve the beauty and diversity of the planet we call home. This love inspires us to live in harmony with nature, to cultivate a deep sense of gratitude and stewardship, and to take action to address the pressing ecological challenges we face.

Moreover, love can be an inward journey of self-discovery and self-acceptance. Self-love is the foundation for a healthy and fulfilling life. It involves cultivating a deep sense of compassion, acceptance, and kindness towards oneself. Self-love allows us to recognize our own worth, prioritize our well-being, and embrace our authentic selves.

Love is a dynamic and evolving force that requires effort, communication, and a willingness to navigate the complexities that arise in relationships. It can be accompanied by feelings of vulnerability, fear, and the potential for heartbreak. However, it is through these challenges that love has the potential to grow stronger, deeper, and more resilient.

Ultimately, love has the power to transform individuals and societies. It can inspire personal growth, promote social harmony, and foster a more compassionate and inclusive world. Love has the capacity to heal wounds, bridge divides, and create a sense of unity and understanding. It is through love that we can build meaningful connections, find purpose and fulfillment, and leave a lasting legacy of compassion and kindness.

In summary, love is a profound and enigmatic force that shapes our lives and the world around us. It is a complex amalgamation of emotions, experiences, and expressions that can manifest in various forms. Love brings joy, meaning, and connection to our lives, and it has the power to inspire personal growth, promote social harmony, and create a more compassionate and inclusive world. Love is the universal language that binds us together as human beings and reminds us of our shared humanity. It is a force that has the capacity to transform us, heal our wounds, and create a world filled with empathy, compassion, and understanding.

Love is the essence of our existence, the guiding light that illuminates our path, and the driving force behind our actions. It is a journey of self-discovery, growth, and transformation that invites us to embrace vulnerability, cultivate compassion, and forge deep connections with others. Love has the power to heal, to inspire, and to create a better world. It is through love that we can transcend our individual differences and come together as a global community, united by our shared humanity and a common desire for peace, understanding, and harmony.

Love is not limited by time or space; it is eternal and transcendent. It has the power to transcend physical boundaries and connect souls across distances. Love can bridge the gap between cultures, languages, and beliefs, bringing people together in a tapestry of unity and understanding.

In the grand tapestry of life, love is the thread that weaves us all together, creating a vibrant and interconnected web of relationships and experiences. It is the force that propels us forward, giving us the strength to overcome obstacles and the courage to pursue our dreams. Love is the fabric of our existence, the heartbeat of humanity, and the essence of what it means to be alive.

In conclusion, love is a boundless and transformative force that has the power to shape our lives and the world around us. It is a complex and multi-faceted emotion that encompasses a wide range of feelings, experiences, and expressions. Love brings joy, meaning, and connection to our lives, and it has the capacity to inspire personal growth, promote social harmony, and create a more compassionate and inclusive world. Love is the universal language that binds us together as human beings, transcending barriers and reminding us of our shared humanity. It is a force that has the capacity to transform us, heal our wounds, and create a world filled with empathy, compassion, and understanding.

Love is the essence of life itself, the very fabric that weaves together the tapestry of our existence. It is the guiding force that allows us to navigate the complexities of the human experience and find meaning and purpose in the world. Love has the power to transcend the limitations of our individuality and connect us to something greater than ourselves. It is through love that we can experience true unity, harmony, and fulfillment.

In the grand symphony of life, love is the melody that resonates in our hearts and souls. It is the rhythm that moves us, the harmony that brings us together, and the crescendo that fills us with awe and wonder. Love is the music that gives color and depth to our existence, making every moment more vibrant and meaningful.

Love is not just a fleeting emotion; it is a state of being. It is a way of living and relating to the world with kindness, compassion, and empathy. Love is a choice we make every day, in every interaction and decision. It is a commitment to treat ourselves and others with respect, understanding, and care.

In the tapestry of love, every thread is important and significant. Each act of love, no matter how small, has the power to create ripples of positivity and transformation. Love is not limited by time or space; it can transcend generations, leaving a lasting legacy of compassion and kindness.

Love is the ultimate truth that binds us all together. It is the common thread that unites us as human beings, reminding us of our shared humanity and interconnectedness. Love is the language that transcends barriers and allows us to communicate beyond words. It is the bridge that connects hearts and minds, creating a sense of belonging and unity.

In the journey of life, love is both the destination and the path. It is the beacon of light that guides us through the darkest of times and the source of strength that empowers us to overcome obstacles. Love is the compass that points us in the direction of our truest selves and the compass that leads us towards a more compassionate, empathetic, and inclusive world.

Love is the greatest gift we can give and receive. It is a treasure that enriches our lives and brings us immeasurable joy. Love is the fuel that ignites our passions and propels us towards our dreams. It is the nourishment that sustains us in times of hardship and the healing balm that soothes our wounds.

In the tapestry of love, each thread is unique and irreplaceable. Every act of love, no matter how small, has the power to make a difference. It is through love that we can create a world that is more compassionate, understanding, and harmonious. Let us embrace the power of love and let it guide us towards a brighter future for all.

Love is the essence of life itself, the very fabric that weaves together the tapestry of our existence. It is the guiding force that allows us to navigate the complexities of the human experience and find meaning and purpose in the world. Love has the power to transcend the limitations of our individuality and connect us to something greater than ourselves. It is through love that we can experience true unity, harmony, and fulfillment.

In the grand symphony of life, love is the melody that resonates in our hearts and souls. It is the rhythm that moves us, the harmony that brings us together, and the crescendo that fills us with awe and wonder. Love is the music that gives color and depth to our existence, making every moment more vibrant and meaningful.

Love is not just a fleeting emotion; it is a state of being. It is a way of living and relating to the world with kindness, compassion, and empathy. Love is a choice we make every day, in every interaction and decision. It is a commitment to treat ourselves and others with respect, understanding, and care.

In the tapestry of love, every thread is important and significant. Each act of love, no matter how small, has the power to create ripples of positivity and transformation. Love is not limited by time or space; it can transcend generations, leaving a lasting legacy of compassion and kindness.

Love is the ultimate truth that binds us all together. It is the common thread that unites us as human beings, reminding us of our shared humanity and interconnectedness. Love is the language that transcends barriers and allows us to communicate beyond words. It is the bridge that connects hearts and minds, creating a sense of belonging and unity.

In the journey of life, love is both the destination and the path. It is the beacon of light that guides us through the darkest of times and the source of strength that empowers us to overcome obstacles. Love is the compass that points us in the direction of our truest selves and the compass that leads us towards a more compassionate, empathetic, and inclusive world.

Love is the greatest gift we can give and receive. It is a treasure that enriches our lives and brings us immeasurable joy. Love is the fuel that ignites our passions and propels us towards our dreams. It is the nourishment that sustains us in times of hardship and the healing balm that soothes our wounds.

In the tapestry of love, each thread is unique and irreplaceable. Every act of love, no matter how small, has the power to make a difference. It is through love that we can create a world that is more compassionate, understanding, and harmonious. Let us embrace the power of love and let it guide us towards a brighter future for all.

Love is the essence of life itself, the very fabric that weaves together the tapestry of our existence. It is the guiding force that allows us to navigate the complexities of the human experience and find meaning and purpose in the world. Love has the power to transcend the limitations of our individuality and connect us to something greater than ourselves. It is through love that we can experience true unity, harmony, and fulfillment.

In the grand symphony of life, love is the melody that resonates in our hearts and souls. It is the rhythm that moves us, the harmony that brings us together, and the crescendo that fills us with awe and wonder. Love is the music that gives color and depth to our existence, making every moment more vibrant and meaningful.

Love is not just a fleeting emotion; it is a state of being. It is a way of living and relating to the world with kindness, compassion, and empathy. Love is a choice we make every day, in every interaction and decision. It is a commitment to treat ourselves and others with respect, understanding, and care.

In the tapestry of love, every thread is important and significant. Each act of love, no matter how small, has the power to create ripples of positivity and transformation. Love is not limited by time or space; it can transcend generations, leaving a lasting legacy of compassion and kindness.

Love is the ultimate truth that binds us all together. It is the common thread that unites us as human beings, reminding us of our shared humanity and interconnectedness. Love is the language that transcends barriers and allows us to communicate beyond words. It is the bridge that connects hearts and minds, creating a sense of belonging and unity.

In the journey of life, love is both the destination and the path. It is the beacon of light that guides us through the darkest of times and the source of strength that empowers us to overcome obstacles. Love is the compass that points us in the direction of our truest selves and the compass that leads us towards a more compassionate, empathetic, and inclusive world.

Love is the greatest gift we can give and receive.

Implementing good intentions

Implementing good intentions involves translating positive thoughts and desires into tangible actions and behaviors. Here are some steps to help implement good intentions:

1. Clarify your intentions: Take the time to reflect on what good intentions mean to you and identify specific areas or actions where you want to make a positive impact. It could be in relationships, personal growth, community service, or any other aspect of life.

2. Set goals: Once you have identified your intentions, set specific and achievable goals that align with them. Break down your goals into smaller, manageable steps that you can work on consistently.

3. Create a plan: Develop a plan of action to implement your good intentions. Determine the practical steps you need to take, the resources or support you may need, and a timeline for achieving your goals.

4. Take action: Start taking concrete steps towards implementing your good intentions. This could involve acts of kindness, volunteering, practicing empathy and compassion, or making positive changes in your behavior and habits.

5. Reflect and adjust: Regularly reflect on your progress and assess how well you are aligning your actions with your intentions. Be open to feedback and adjust your approach if necessary. Celebrate your successes and learn from any setbacks or challenges.

6. Practice self-care: Taking care of your own well-being is essential for implementing good intentions effectively. Make sure to prioritize self-care, maintain a healthy work-life

balance, and seek support when needed.

7. Stay committed: Implementing good intentions requires consistent effort and commitment. Stay motivated by reminding yourself of the positive impact your actions can have and the values that drive your intentions.

Remember, implementing good intentions is an ongoing process that requires patience, perseverance, and self-reflection. By taking deliberate actions aligned with your positive intentions, you can make a meaningful difference in your own life and the lives of others.

Self-control is a complex and multifaceted aspect of human behavior that influences various aspects of our lives. It encompasses a wide range of cognitive, emotional, and behavioral processes that allow us to regulate and manage our thoughts, feelings, and actions in order to achieve desired outcomes and resist immediate temptations.

At its core, self-control involves making deliberate decisions and exerting willpower to override impulsive urges or reactions. It requires us to consider the long-term consequences and benefits of our actions, rather than being driven solely by immediate gratification or impulses. Self-control enables us to delay gratification, resist temptations, and make choices that align with our values and goals.

One key element of self-control is the ability to manage our thoughts and cognitive processes. This includes maintaining focus, resisting distractions, and staying committed to our goals. Self-control allows us to overcome procrastination, maintain concentration, and effectively manage our time and resources. It helps us resist the allure of short-term pleasures and make choices that contribute to our long-term success and well-being.

Self-control also plays a significant role in managing our emotions. It involves recognizing and understanding our feelings and being able to regulate them in a healthy and adaptive way. Self-control enables us to control anger, manage stress, and respond to challenging situations with composure and resilience. It allows us to navigate through emotional ups and downs with greater stability and make thoughtful decisions rather than being driven solely by our emotions.

Furthermore, self-control extends to our behaviors and habits. It involves resisting immediate temptations and making choices that align with our values and long-term goals. This can include adhering to a healthy lifestyle, such as maintaining a balanced diet, exercising regularly, and getting enough sleep. Self-control empowers us to resist harmful behaviors, such as smoking or excessive drinking, and make choices that contribute to our overall physical and mental well-being.

In addition, self-control plays a critical role in decision-making and impulse control. It allows us to evaluate the potential risks and rewards of different choices, weigh the long-term implications, and make decisions that align with our values and aspirations. Self-control helps us resist impulsive actions or decisions that may have negative consequences and make choices that are in our best interest in the long run.

Developing and maintaining self-control is a lifelong journey that requires self-awareness, discipline, and practice. It involves recognizing our triggers and vulnerabilities, setting clear goals, and implementing strategies to effectively manage our impulses. This can include techniques such as mindfulness, meditation, and cognitive reframing, which help us cultivate self-awareness and make intentional choices.

It is important to note that self-control is not about being perfect or denying ourselves all pleasures. It is about finding a balance and making intentional choices that promote our overall well-being and personal growth. Self-control allows us to make choices that align with our values, prioritize our long-term goals, and contribute to our overall happiness and success.

In conclusion, self-control is a fundamental aspect of human behavior that encompasses various cognitive, emotional, and behavioral processes. It enables us to regulate and manage our thoughts, emotions, and actions in order to make positive choices and achieve our long-term goals. By cultivating self-control, we can navigate through life's challenges with resilience, make choices that align with our values, and lead fulfilling and purposeful lives.

The Best of Humans

"The best of humans" is an awe-inspiring concept that celebrates the limitless potential and remarkable qualities that define our shared humanity. It encapsulates the highest ideals, virtues, and aspirations that inspire us to strive for greatness and make a lasting impact on the world.

At its core, the best of humans is rooted in love, the universal force that connects us all. Love encompasses boundless compassion, empathy, and a deep sense of care for others. It is the driving force behind acts of kindness, generosity, and selflessness. Love transcends boundaries, unites diverse individuals, and creates a sense of belonging and unity. It is through love that we can build a world filled with understanding, harmony, and compassion.

Kindness is a powerful pillar of the best of humans. It is the conscious choice to extend warmth, empathy, and goodwill to others. Kindness can be expressed through simple gestures of courtesy, a listening ear, or acts of service that brighten someone's day. It has the transformative power to uplift spirits, heal wounds, and foster a sense of community. Kindness is a reflection of our inherent goodness and the capacity to make a positive difference in the lives of others.

Compassion is intimately intertwined with the best of humans. It is the ability to deeply understand and share in the suffering of others. Compassion moves us to take action, to alleviate pain, and to advocate for justice and equality. It is the foundation of empathy, allowing us to connect with others on a profound level and to extend a helping hand to those in need. Compassion fuels our desire to create a better world for all.

Courage stands as a defining characteristic of the best of humans. It is the strength to confront fear, overcome obstacles, and stand up for what is right, even in the face of adversity. Courageous individuals inspire others through their bold actions, unwavering convictions, and willingness to challenge the status quo. They demonstrate resilience, inspiring us to face our own fears and embrace change in pursuit of a brighter future.

Integrity is an essential attribute that defines the best of humans. It is the unwavering commitment to honesty, ethics, and moral principles. Individuals with integrity demonstrate consistency, authenticity, and accountability in their actions. They inspire trust, respect, and admiration through their unwavering adherence to their values and their dedication to doing what is right, even when it is difficult.

Wisdom is another hallmark of the best of humans. It is the ability to discern truth, make sound judgments, and apply knowledge with compassion and understanding. Wise individuals possess deep insight and perspective, allowing them to navigate life's complexities with grace and humility. They serve as beacons of guidance, inspiring others with their profound understanding and ability to make meaningful contributions to society.

The best of humans is also characterized by resilience, the capacity to bounce back from adversity and grow stronger in the face of challenges. Resilient individuals find strength, determination, and purpose in the face of setbacks. They inspire others through their ability to overcome obstacles, adapt to change, and find meaning in difficult circumstances. Resilience ignites hope and empowers us to persevere in the pursuit of our goals.

Moreover, the best of humans encompasses qualities such as humility, forgiveness, gratitude, creativity, and a commitment to continuous learning. It is an ongoing journey of self-discovery, growth, and transformation. The best of humans calls us to embrace our imperfections, learn from our mistakes, and cultivate a deep sense of gratitude for the blessings in our lives. It encourages us to tap into our creativity, embrace curiosity, and foster a lifelong love of learning.

In conclusion, the best of humans represents the pinnacle of human potential, virtue, and character. It is a profound reminder of the immense capacity for goodness that resides within each of us. The best of humans calls us to embody love, kindness, compassion, courage, integrity, wisdom, resilience, and countless other qualities that inspire us to make a positive impact on the world. By embracing the best of humans within ourselves and in our interactions with others, we can contribute to a more compassionate, just, and harmonious world for all.

Living Content in a Storm

In the Bible, there is a powerful story about Jesus and his disciples being caught in a fierce storm while crossing the Sea of Galilee. As the wind howled and the waves crashed against their small boat, the disciples became fearful for their lives. Amidst the chaos and uncertainty, Jesus remained calm and composed.

In that moment, Jesus spoke with authority and said, "Peace! Be still!" Instantly, the wind ceased, and the waves became calm. This miraculous event not only demonstrated Jesus' power over the forces of nature, but it also carried a profound message about finding contentment in the midst of life's storms.

Jesus' words "Peace! Be still!" were not only a command to the wind and the waves, but also an invitation to the disciples to find peace within themselves. It was a reminder to trust in God's sovereignty and to have faith in His ability to bring calmness and tranquility to even the most turbulent situations.

Through this story, Jesus teaches us the importance of cultivating inner peace and contentment, even when we find ourselves in the midst of life's storms. He shows us that true peace comes from surrendering our fears and worries to God and trusting in His divine plan and providence.

Being content in a storm does not mean denying or ignoring the challenges we face. It is not about pretending that everything is fine when it is not. Instead, it is about finding a deep sense of peace and trust in God's presence and guidance, even in the midst of difficulties.

When we choose to be content in a storm, we are acknowledging that God is with us, and that He is in control. We are surrendering our worries and fears to Him, and allowing His peace to fill our hearts and minds. This inner peace enables us to face the storm with courage, resilience, and faith, knowing that God is working all things together for our good.

Jesus' words about being content in a storm remind us that storms are temporary. They may be intense and challenging, but they do not last forever. By holding onto our faith and finding peace within ourselves, we can weather the storm and emerge stronger on the other side.

Moreover, Jesus' example of being content in a storm extends beyond just physical storms. It speaks to the storms of life that we all face - the storms of uncertainty, loss, disappointment, and heartache. In these moments, Jesus invites us to find solace in His presence, to trust in His promises, and to rely on His strength.

Finding contentment in a storm requires a shift in perspective. It involves focusing on the eternal truths and promises of God, rather than being consumed by the temporary circumstances. It means choosing to hold onto hope, even when everything around us seems bleak. It means finding peace in the midst of chaos, knowing that God is with us and that He will never leave us nor forsake us.

In our own lives, we often experience storms that threaten to overwhelm us - whether they are physical, emotional, or spiritual. These storms can take the form of personal hardships, relationship challenges, health issues, or financial struggles. In these moments, Jesus' words serve as a guiding light, reminding us to seek contentment and peace in Him.

When we are content in a storm, we are not defined by our circumstances, but by our unwavering trust in God's goodness and faithfulness. We draw strength from knowing that God is in control, that He has a purpose for our lives, and that He will carry us through the storm to the other side.

Furthermore, being content in a storm allows us to discover the lessons and growth opportunities that arise from difficult situations. It is in the midst of storms that our character is shaped, our faith is deepened, and our resilience is tested. By finding contentment and peace in the storm, we open ourselves up to the transformative work of God in our lives.

In the story of Jesus calming the storm, we see that the disciples went from being filled with fear to being filled with awe and wonder at Jesus' power and authority. Similarly, when we find contentment in the midst of life's storms, we can experience a profound transformation within ourselves. We can move from a place of fear and anxiety to a place of trust and peace.

In conclusion, Jesus' command to "Peace! Be still!" in the midst of a storm serves as a powerful reminder for us to find contentment and inner peace in the face of life's challenges. By trusting in God's sovereignty, surrendering our fears to Him, and cultivating a deep sense of peace within ourselves, we can navigate through the storms of life with faith, resilience, and hope. Jesus' example teaches us that even in the midst of the fiercest storms, we can find calmness and contentment by anchoring ourselves in His love and presence. As we embrace this mindset, we can not only survive the storms of life but also emerge stronger, wiser, and more compassionate on the other side. The story of Jesus calming the storm is a timeless reminder that in Him, we can find true peace and contentment, regardless of the storms we face.

Perseverance

Perseverance, the remarkable and awe-inspiring quality that resides deep within the human spirit, is an extraordinary force that propels individuals to overcome obstacles, conquer adversity, and achieve greatness. It is a testament to the indomitable will, unwavering determination, and relentless pursuit of excellence that sets apart those who persevere from those who give up.

At its core, perseverance is the unwavering commitment to stay the course, no matter how challenging or daunting the path may be. It is the refusal to succumb to adversity, the resilience to bounce back from failure, and the unwavering resolve to press forward, even when the odds seem insurmountable. Perseverance is the driving force that fuels individuals to rise above their circumstances, shatter barriers, and achieve extraordinary feats that surpass the limitations of human potential.

One of the defining characteristics of perseverance is the ability to maintain unwavering focus and determination in the face of adversity. It is the mental fortitude to overcome self-doubt, fear, and uncertainty, and to stay true to one's goals and aspirations in the midst of immense challenges. Perseverance empowers individuals to push through the most grueling moments, knowing that their efforts and sacrifices will ultimately lead to success. It is the unwavering belief in the power of their dreams that propels them forward, even when the road ahead is filled with obstacles.

Furthermore, perseverance is intimately connected to resilience—the remarkable capacity to bounce back from setbacks, learn from failures, and adapt to changing circumstances. It is the ability to navigate through the darkest valleys and emerge stronger and more resilient on the other side. Perseverance enables individuals to transform setbacks into stepping stones on the path to success, embracing them as opportunities for growth, self-improvement, and character development. It is the understanding that failure is not the end but a necessary part of the journey towards achieving greatness.

Another crucial aspect of perseverance is the ability to maintain a positive mindset and unwavering optimism, even in the face of overwhelming adversity. It is the unshakeable belief that success is not only possible but inevitable, regardless of the obstacles that may arise. Perseverance empowers individuals to see setbacks as temporary roadblocks rather than permanent barriers, fueling their determination to overcome them and continue blazing their trail towards their goals. It is the unwavering faith in their own abilities and the belief that every challenge is an opportunity for growth and transformation.

Moreover, perseverance is characterized by adaptability and flexibility—the willingness to adjust strategies, embrace new approaches, and navigate uncharted territories when faced with unexpected challenges. It is the recognition that the journey towards success is rarely a linear path, and that detours, redirections, and course corrections may be necessary along the way. Perseverance allows individuals to be open-minded, innovative, and resourceful in finding alternative routes to their objectives, never losing sight of their ultimate destination. It is the ability to adapt to changing circumstances, evolve with the demands of the journey, and seize opportunities for growth and progress.

Perseverance is also nurtured and strengthened by a supportive community. Surrounding oneself with like-minded individuals, mentors, and allies can provide invaluable encouragement, guidance, and inspiration during the most challenging of times. It is through the collective support of others that individuals find the unwavering strength, motivation, and accountability to persevere, knowing that they are not alone in their journey and that their triumphs will inspire and uplift others. The power of a supportive community is a catalyst for perseverance, fostering an environment of collaboration, growth, and shared success.

In conclusion, perseverance is a truly extraordinary quality that encompasses unwavering determination, resilience, adaptability, unwavering optimism, and an unrelenting belief in one's abilities. It is the force that empowers individuals to overcome seemingly insurmountable obstacles, learn from failures, and transcend their limitations to achieve greatness. Perseverance is not just about reaching the pinnacle of success but also about the personal growth, resilience, character development, and transformation that occur along the arduous yet immensely rewarding journey.

As we embrace the power of perseverance, we unlock our true potential and inspire others to do the same. We become beacons of light, guiding others through the darkest of times and showing them that the impossible is indeed possible. The journey of perseverance is not for the faint of heart—it requires unwavering dedication, unyielding determination, and relentless pursuit of excellence. But in the end, it is through perseverance that we discover our true strength, unleash our full potential, and create a lasting impact on the world around us.

So let us embark on this incredible journey of perseverance, knowing that with every step we take, we are one step closer to achieving greatness and leaving an indelible legacy for generations to come. Together, we can inspire a world where perseverance is not just a quality but a way of life, where individuals embrace challenges with unwavering determination, and where the human spirit triumphs over every obstacle, no matter how formidable. Let us be the torchbearers of perseverance, igniting a flame of resilience and determination that will illuminate the path for all who follow.

Blessing

A blessing is a deeply profound and universally cherished concept that spans across cultures, religions, and traditions. It is a sacred act or words spoken with the intention of invoking divine grace, favor, and protection upon someone or something. The essence of a blessing lies in its ability to transcend the boundaries of the physical world and tap into the realm of the spiritual, connecting individuals to a higher power and fostering a sense of divine guidance and support.

In its purest form, a blessing is an expression of goodwill, love, and positive energy that seeks to bring forth blessings and positive outcomes in various aspects of life. It is a heartfelt invocation that draws upon the infinite power of the divine to shower blessings upon the recipient, enveloping them in a cloak of divine favor, benevolence, and protection.

Blessings hold immense significance in religious and spiritual contexts, where they are often bestowed by spiritual leaders, clergy, or elders who are seen as conduits between the earthly realm and the divine. Through prayers, rituals, or specific words and actions, these blessings are invoked to invite and harness divine intervention, wisdom, and support. They are seen as a means to establish a deep and meaningful connection with the divine, seeking its guidance, providence, and blessings in all endeavors.

The act of receiving a blessing is a sacred and transformative experience. It is a moment of profound connection and alignment with the divine, wherein the recipient is enveloped in the loving embrace of the divine presence. A blessing is believed to bestow divine grace, protection, and favor upon the individual, infusing their life with positive energy, well-being, and spiritual growth. It serves as a reminder of the interconnectedness between the human and divine realms, fostering a sense of purpose, hope, and transcendence.

Blessings can take various forms, each holding its own unique significance. Individual blessings are often bestowed upon a person, invoking divine favor, success, and protection in their personal journey. Family blessings seek to extend divine blessings and harmony to the entire family unit, nurturing love, unity, and prosperity. Community blessings are offered to groups or communities, aiming to invoke divine favor, unity, and well-being among its members.

In addition to personal blessings, objects, places, and events can also be blessed. Religious artifacts or sacred items are often blessed to imbue them with spiritual power, sanctity, and significance. Special occasions, such as weddings, births, or new ventures, can be blessed to ensure a positive and auspicious beginning, inviting divine blessings and support.

Beyond religious and spiritual contexts, blessings can be found in everyday life, where they are expressed as acts of kindness, support, or well-wishes towards others. Offering a heartfelt blessing to someone can be a way to show care, empathy, and a desire for their well-being. It can serve as a source of encouragement, inspiration, and upliftment, creating a positive and harmonious atmosphere.

Blessings are believed to have profound effects on the recipients. They are seen as a means of invoking divine favor, protection, and guidance. Blessings are often associated with positive outcomes, such as good health, success, abundance, and spiritual growth. They can inspire hope, boost morale, and instill a sense of purpose and direction. The divine energy and grace invoked through a blessing have the power to transform lives, bringing about personal growth, healing, and a deep sense of connection to the divine.

Moreover, blessings have a transformative power that extends beyond the individual level. They foster a sense of unity, interconnectedness, and community. When blessings are shared, they create a ripple effect, spreading positivity, love, and harmony among individuals and society at large. They serve as a catalyst for compassion, understanding, and collective well-being.

Receiving or giving a blessing can be a deeply humbling and gratitude-inducing experience. It acknowledges the presence of divine love and support in one's life and serves as a reminder of the interconnectedness between individuals, communities, and the divine. It cultivates a sense of gratitude, reverence, and awe for the divine blessings bestowed upon us, encouraging us to share those blessings with others and create a world filled with love, compassion, and harmony.

In conclusion, blessings hold immense significance as acts or words that invoke divine grace, favor, and protection. They are expressions of goodwill, love, and positive energy that seek to bring forth positive outcomes, spiritual connection, and well-being. Whether given in religious or everyday contexts, blessings have the power to uplift, inspire, and foster a sense of gratitude, hope, unity, and spiritual growth. They establish a sacred bond between the recipient and the divine, igniting a transformative journey of well-being, purpose, and transcendence.

By embracing the power of blessings and incorporating them into our lives, we can cultivate a deep sense of connection to the divine, tap into the infinite wellspring of divine wisdom and support, and experience the profound transformation that comes from aligning ourselves with the divine purpose. May we be open to receiving and sharing blessings, spreading love, positivity, and harmony throughout the world, and creating a collective reality where the divine presence is felt by all.

We truly hope you have enjoyed this book.

C.W. Fortney & Kristal J. Smith

But their world is rocked by the arrival of Gabriel, a charismatic musician with a troubled past of his own. As Gabriel's music weaves its spell over Mia, she finds herself torn between the allure of his carefree lifestyle and the stability offered by Liam's unwavering support.

As Mia grapples with her inner turmoil, she is confronted with the harsh realities of addiction—a cycle of highs and lows, moments of clarity followed by lapses into darkness. But with Liam by her side, she begins to unravel the tangled web of her past, confronting long-buried traumas and finding solace in the power of forgiveness.

Meanwhile, Gabriel's presence serves as a catalyst for change, challenging Mia to confront her demons head-on and reclaim control of her destiny. Yet, as their bond deepens, Mia is forced to confront the painful truth: that love alone may not be enough to overcome the grip of addiction.

As Mia's journey unfolds, "Echoes of the Heart" explores the complex interplay between addiction and the human heart—the ache of longing, the ecstasy of connection, and the enduring hope for redemption. Through moments of triumph and despair, Mia discovers that true healing lies not in escaping her past, but in embracing it with courage and compassion.

Ultimately, "Echoes of the Heart" is a testament to the resilience of the human spirit—a reminder that even in our darkest moments, we possess the strength to rise above our circumstances and forge a path toward redemption. And as Mia's story unfolds, readers are invited to embark on their own journey of self-discovery, finding solace and inspiration in the universal truths that bind us all together.

As readers turn the final page of "Echoes of the Heart," they are left with a profound sense of hope—that no matter how far we may stray from the path, the light of love and redemption will always guide us home. And with AIERA2024.com, readers can continue to explore the themes of addiction, resilience, and the human heart, forging connections and fostering understanding in a world that is ever-changing and endlessly complex.

Don't miss out!

Visit the website below and you can sign up to receive emails whenever C.W. Fortney publishes a new book. There's no charge and no obligation.

https://books2read.com/r/B-A-XIMCB-KIQAD

BOOKS2READ

Connecting independent readers to independent writers.

About the Author

C.W. Fortney
Read more at www.AIERA2024.com.

About the Publisher

Charles W. Fortney
Student Ambassador Capellla University